# Fighter Squadron
## at
# Guadalcanal

G·K
Hall
&Co.

*Also by Max Brand
in Large Print:*


The Hair Trigger Kid
The Bells of San Filipo
The Black Rider and Other Stories
Clung
The Ghost Wagon and Other Great Western
   Adventures
Gunman's Legacy
Murder Me!
Rippon Rides Double
The Secret of Dr. Kildare
Sixteen in Nome
Free Range Lanning
The Return of Free Range Lanning
Ronicky Doone's Reward

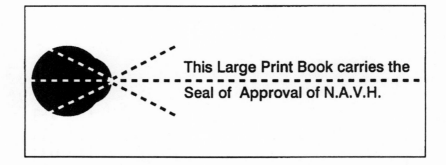

This Large Print Book carries the
Seal of Approval of N.A.V.H.

# Fighter Squadron
## at
# Guadalcanal

# Max Brand

G.K. Hall & Co.
Thorndike, Maine

Published in 1997 by arrangement with Naval Institute Press.

G.K. Hall Large Print Paperback Collection.

The text of this Large Print edition is unabridged.
Other aspects of the book may vary from the original edition.

Set in 16 pt. Plantin by Al Chase.

Printed in the United States on permanent paper.

---

**Library of Congress Cataloging in Publication Data**

Brand, Max, 1892–1944.
    Fighter Squadron at Guadalcanal / Max Brand.
      p.   cm.
    ISBN 0-7838-8103-7  (lg. print : sc)
    1. World War, 1939–1945 — Aerial operations, American.
  2. World War, 1939–1945 — Personal narratives, American.
  3. United States. Marine Corps — Aviation — History.
  4. United States. Marine Fighter Squadron, 212th — History.
  5. World War, 1939–1945 — Campaigns — Soloman Islands
— Guadalcanal Island.  6. Large type books.  7. Guadalcanal
Island (Soloman Islands) — History, Military.  I.  Title.
  [D790.B65   1997]
  940.54′4973—dc21                        97-3440

To the men of Marine Fighter Squadron 212
and all those who fought with them
at Guadalcanal

# Contents

# Introduction

I first met the author of this book at Laguna Beach near Los Angeles one evening early in 1943. Several other Marine airmen and myself from the El Toro base not far away had been given use of a beach house by its somewhat nervous owner, who had visions of it being shelled by Japanese submarines then active off the coast. We were members of the 212th Marine Fighter Squadron, recently returned from South Pacific duty culminating in the struggle against the Japanese for the strategic island of Guadalcanal; and now we were told that the famous author "Max Brand," whose real name was Frederick Faust, author of *Destry Rides Again*, the Dr. Kildare stories, and many others, wanted to interview us for a book based on our experiences in combat.

Since I had taken command of the squadron after we lost our courageous leader, Joe Bauer, during the fighting at Guadalcanal, I was especially interested in meeting Faust and helping him with his book. As he entered the room that evening I was aware of a massive figure standing about six feet three, weighing maybe 220 pounds. He wore a rumpled gray suit, white shirt with tie, and had a rich, deep voice and a straightforward manner.

He got right down to business with his portable typewriter on a coffee table between us and asked me questions, typing out my answers rapidly with two fingers. I was impressed by the seriousness and intelligence of his questioning and his enthusiasm for what we were doing. Our working session lasted an hour or more and was duplicated with three of my fellow squadron members, using up most of that Saturday night, though we had time for a few beers before morning.

At his home in the Brentwood suburb of Los Angeles, Faust interviewed many other members of the 212th, ground crew as well as pilots, because, as he said, he wanted readers to get a complete understanding of the men who composed the squadron, of their thoughts and feelings as well as their actions before, during, and after combat.

I learned later that he was taking time from very pressing and much more lucrative work in order to spend many hours conducting these interviews, and then writing a book he hoped would give the home-front reading public a true picture of war, while at the same time he was trying to get an assignment as a combat correspondent — despite his fifty-one years and bad heart — that would put him in closer personal touch with warfare. He got his assignment and left suddenly for North Africa before he could oversee publication of his manuscript. He was killed May 12, 1944, on the Italian Front while accompanying an infantry platoon in a night attack against a strong German position, as correspondent for *Harper's Magazine* and *The Infantry Journal.*

When Faust lost his life in the battle of Santa Maria Infante, it seemed, according to his surviving daughter, that the war book he'd hoped to write about Americans in combat was lost with him. But meanwhile the war book he had already written, this one, was in a sense going underground. In the confusion of those wartime years and of his death, it was lost sight of and all but forgotten by family members and by his literary executors. But he had given a copy of his manuscript to Captain, later Major, Mel Freeman, one of the 212th pilots he interviewed. Years later Freeman, based in San Francisco, made a copy for his fellow 212th pilot Colonel Frank C. Drury, then living in Florida. Drury eventually passed his copy along to me here in California, where through a fortunate series of circumstances contact was made with Faust's daughter, Jane Faust Easton, in Santa Barbara. She discovered she had a somewhat different manuscript of the "Marines Book," as she called it.

All of us working together, including Naval Air Reserve Flight Engineer Robert Andrade, whose printing class at Palm Springs High School had set a souvenir version in type as part of their classwork, have produced this book, lost for half a century and now rediscovered. It is Frederick Faust's only book of nonfiction and is his wartime

11

legacy to his country and to readers worldwide.

*Fighter Squadron at Guadalcanal,* as you will find, is written in the language and attitudes of wartime 1943. Though they may at times seem strange or even shocking, I can say from personal experience that they are truly representative of their time and circumstances.

This is in the full sense a war book. It is about men locked in deadly combat. It is about Americans engaged in a global struggle for survival against Hitler, Mussolini, and Japanese imperialist aggression as embodied by General Hideki Tojo, Japan's wartime premier. It is about a future that we enjoy now but which then seemed very uncertain. Perhaps above all it is simply a narrative of human beings under great stress, told largely in their own words in a manner that present-day readers, whatever their experience, may find revealing and informative.

*Brigadier General F. R. Payne, USMC (Ret.)*

# Historical Note

*Fighter Squadron at Guadalcanal* is probably the last contemporary account we will have of the war in the Pacific. Lost for over fifty years after the author's tragic death while covering the Italian campaign, the book deserves a place alongside other classics of the early war years, such as Richard Tregaskis's *Guadalcanal Diary*, John Hersey's *Into the Valley*, Ira Wolfert's *Battle for the Solomons*, and Stanley Johnston's *The Grim Reapers*.

The purpose of the few annotations sprinkled through the text is to provide either historical accuracy or pertinent supplementary information. Frederick Faust, writing here as "Max Brand," did not attempt a comprehensive history of air warfare over Guadalcanal or of Marine Corps aviation in the Solomons campaign, neither of which could have been accurately accomplished in 1943. Instead he wisely concentrated on small-unit history to convey the flavor of the often bizarre, always exhausting war that both sides waged on and over the most important island of World War II.

Despite the inevitable discrepancies in fact and interpretation, *Fighter Squadron at Guadalcanal* holds up remarkably well as combat history when checked with later, more detailed and authoritative accounts, including Richard Frank's *Guadalcanal*, John Lundstrom's *The First Team and the Guadalcanal Campaign*, Robert Sherrod's *History of Marine Corps Aviation in World War II*, Samuel Eliot Morison's volume on Guadalcanal in his *History of United States Naval Operations in World War II*, and Robert Leckie's *Challenge for the Pacific*. Faust's book also complements broader studies of the entire Pacific war, including Ronald Spector's *Eagle against the Sun* and John Costello's *The Pacific War*.

As with many, if not most, contemporary accounts of the Pacific war, Faust's book is racist, reflecting the opinions and attitudes of his subjects and his fellow citizens. As Spector and others have demonstrated, both sides waged war with hatred and fanaticism. Each detested the other as racially inferior. Sanitizing such truths does not serve either history or present attempts to surmount such puerile, destructive thinking. Like all of us, Faust was a product of his times, and those times, as he so convincingly conveys, were both desperate and exalted.

*Lisle A. Rose*

# The Forward Echelon

## one

These young Marines sit opposite my typewriter, here in Los Angeles in 1943. Home on leave from battle, they are giving me their precious time before they go back again to the front lines. Sometimes what they say goes down on paper word for word, sometimes in notes. This is their narrative. I am simply the voice through which they speak.

There was a revolution in the South Pacific island of New Caledonia a year ago when the Free French overthrew the Vichyite supporters of Hitler and of Tojo, Japan's wartime premier. After that, the Free French controlled the New Hebrides, and it was safe to land American troops. It was necessary to act quickly in order to establish some sort of position before the Japanese arrived from the north; but those days were still close to the Pearl Harbor attack, ships and men were hard to find, and the High Command, looking anxiously over available material, spotted an American convoy already deep in the South Seas.[1]

On March 20, 1942, the U.S. transport *Crescent*

*City*, below the equator and bound for Tonga, received orders to change course for the island of Efate in the New Hebrides. That morning at seven o'clock the loudspeakers throughout the ship carried word of the change of the Forward Echelon of Marine Aircraft Group 24, under command of Captain John K. Little. There was a general reaching for maps. "New Hebrides" was a name without meaning, "Efate" seemed a misspelling, and no one could give much information. One thing was made clear by the maps, however: Efate was up there near the danger line which the Japs were running across the Pacific as they struck south toward Australia. The *Crescent City*, ancient and battle-scarred from the Pearl Harbor attack, had been plenty good enough to take them down to Tonga's white beaches and lazy days, but it seemed like a helpless old tub to be pointed at the new destination. From that moment, tension began to build among the Marines on board. Two destroyers and a cruiser were guarding the convoy, still they seemed naked and out in the rain. But that is what the United States Marines are meant for: not the massive strokes of war but the far-flung missions, the quick blows, the surprise attacks, the bitter work of establishing beachheads.

There were 152 of these Marines under the command of Captain Little and of the flight surgeon who was to become his right-hand man in the tough days that followed, Navy Lieutenant Marion Martin. Captain Little was a two-fisted, red-faced Missourian, an engineer of anything from a steel bridge to madame's dainty summer house, a man of patience, a resolute workman, a lifter of weights. The doctor was his opposite, a soft-speaking Southerner with a dark, beautiful face and a mind never at rest, draining the strength from his body but never quite exhausting the batteries of nerve energy. These were the two who would work hand in glove to the end.

Their men were specially chosen. When Colonel Larkin decided to send out this mission, he told Colonel Kimes that he could have his pick of the Marines in the Pearl Harbor area, and Kimes had not reached blindly into the grab bag. He gathered up a lot of technicians and mechanics with brains in their heads as well as in their hands. They were regulars, and some had done duty in China, Wake, Guam, Midway, and other outposts of the Marine Corps, but the great majority were new enlistments, keen, eager to learn, but in great need of teaching.[2] They were part of the great improvisation with which this democracy was trying to prepare itself for total war, and Sergeant Major Earl Ross looked on them grimly and with some despair. Between these men and Captain Little, who was totally new to the unit, Ross was the intermediary and connecting link, an old-line Marine as smooth in his ways as a sea lion in the sea, but with the bark and bite that are necessary in the ideal "top-kick."

To him the Marine Corps was a career, and he had risen through the ranks when it took two

17

years of study and good performance for a recruit to become a corporal. A good Marine sergeant of the old line was capable of putting a whole company through its paces in any sort of a pinch, with a vocabulary hot enough to weld armor plate. Sergeant Major Ross was a sample.

"A Marine doesn't have to be very big, but he always has to be big enough. The saying is that a good Marine is equal parts mule and tiger; you should be able to fatten him on hardtack, water, and red pepper; he is enclosed in sharkskin that the sun cannot blister and rocks cannot scratch; and he is born to give more than he takes."

These were some of the thoughts behind the eyes of the sergeant major as he looked over the forward echelon. The old hands were well enough, but the new men had far to go. However, their spirit was willing, their flesh was not weak, and the proof of the pudding would be the eating.

Fortunately, he thought, the new commander of the outfit, Captain Little, was a reserve officer who'd done a lot of military living and thinking ever since he attended the Wentworth Military Academy, and the spirit of the sergeant major fitted his beliefs the way music fits the words of a song. To an officer, a new organization is like a foreign language: it has to be learned. And Ross was the perfect interpreter. Before the voyage ended, Little knew the key men in the echelon — which meant that he was ready to put it to work.

In the meantime, the convoy was nearing Efate,

the unknown. It was comprised of a tanker laden with invaluable aviation gasoline, a cargo ship, and the transport, which carried, besides the echelon, the Fourth Marine Defense Battalion of seven hundred men and officers, a unit high in firepower with coastal-defense guns and 3-inch anti-aircraft rifles. As the *Crescent City* sailed deeper into dangerous waters, the captain of the ship ordered the gasoline to be drained from the amphibious Duck which the forward echelon was bringing along. The plane was to be the eyes of the unit while it was on the island, but now the life was drained out of it for fear of Jap bombs or torpedoes. A Jap carrier in fact had been spotted not very far from the *Crescent City* on March 21.[3] Captain Little took charge of the camouflaging of the ship with nets and whatever could be used to block out shadow lines so as to obscure it from air observation; but no Jap planes came over. However, if the danger was not in the air, it was in the sea. A few evenings later, at the close of the day when a ship is silhouetted as a perfect target against the horizon, a sailor on a convoying ship spotted a periscope, and throughout the *Crescent City* sounded the sharp little toot-toot-toot-toot which meant battle stations. The ship rocked. One of the lieutenants in Little's cabin was sure that a torpedo had struck home; however, it was only the destroyers dropping depth charges.

That was the last excitement until they picked up the British and Australian escort. In the far background was a powerful British fleet, its vessels painted with a zigzag camouflage pattern of white lines on gray, a clumsy measure as old as the first world war. But that didn't keep the boys from cheering, because two of the ships were the *Achilles* and *Leander*, which had closed with the mighty German battleship *Graf Spee* off the South American coast in the early months of this second world war and worried her to death with their little 6-inch shells. Both of them had come away with gaping holes in their sides.[4] Now proudly wearing their steel patches, they ran on with the convoy until about noon of March 29, when Captain Little had his first look at Efate, turning from horizon-blue to brown to green.

The tall palms bending and the native women in calico dresses along the shore, the idle, amorous illusions about South Sea islands and the sense of freedom that comes from being near the end of the world, made Efate look like a very lovely green slice of destiny indeed.

"We thought we were out of school. So far away nobody would care what we did. We thought we were playing hooky. But we were the ones that were hooked. And gaffed, too. We were going to stick there month after month, in a fine, slippery, wet hell with the mosquitoes sounding off like air-raid sirens. We were right up there under Tojo's chin. If he only opened his mouth, we'd fall in. A couple of Jap destroyers could have cleaned us out almost any time. That's what it meant being a forward echelon. We were for war, all right. We were right on the edge of the falling-off place."

Little, standing on the forward deck, watched the shore coming toward him so slowly that he knew the captain was feeling his way into an uncharted harbor, making continual soundings. To Commander Reeves, a medical officer of long service, Little said with enthusiasm, "It looks fine, doesn't it?"

"Does it to you?" said Reeves. "It looks sick to me."

But after all, Port Vila was a pretty place — from a distance. There were coral outcrops, oyster white among the coconut palms; flags flew over the white houses of the British and French commissioners; and there was a scattering of red-roofed native shacks. "A lot of things were hidden behind those cosmetics," said Little.

As the ship anchored — two miles from shore was the closest it could come — a small boat approached flying the insignia of the Royal Australian Air Force. Flight Officer Sands came on board with others and received a volley of questions at once. Had there been any Jap air reconnaissance? Had Jap submarines been watching the island? Then, above all, Was there an airfield?

There was not; and that was the answer which had the most weight and sting to it, for Little knew that he had barely men and equipment enough to keep an established field in working order. Vaguely, like mountains seen at twilight, he began to guess at the dimensions of a job too big to name, too big to make good sense. The vision frightened him. He put it out of his mind. Skipper Kiland of the *Crescent City*, a reserve full captain of the Old Navy, called a meeting of the department heads to discuss plans for unloading the ship. His idea was to rush everything at full speed. If he delayed in unloading his cargo, Jap aircraft or subs might sneak in with a fatal counterblow. He must heap everything headlong on the beach and then rush back north and west for another shipment. In the ship-famine, cargo space meant more than gold. Just how fast could that unloading be done? Our Allies on the island knew how long it took to freight in the tonnage of a big ship on small lighters, and they suggested that a month or six weeks would be the minimum requirement — a suggestion that heightened Captain Kiland's blood pressure and warmed his vocabulary.

In the British paddock on a grassy hill overlooking the harbor, the eight hundred men from the *Crescent City* were bivouacked with a hasty installation of anti-aircraft guns and other pieces to command the harbor. The men were divided into shifts of two hundred "longshoremen," each working the twenty-four hours through and driving all the time. The job was big. Aside from the massive weight of coastal guns, tractors, and trucks, there were masses of provisions to handle, and approximately eighty thousand gallons of aviation gas had to be pumped into fifty-five-gallon drums. The first piece of equipment that went over the side was the precious Duck, the J2F-5, which at once taxied off to a secret rendezvous at Royal Australian Air Force headquarters. The South Sea Island Traders loaned floats with which copra was handled between freighters and shore. Many pieces of heavy equipment went in on tank landing barges. And to help everything forward, there were three days without a drop of rain. That was about the only bit of good luck that came to the echelon on Efate. And in five days from anchoring, the convoy was unloaded. Captain Kiland could steam off again to pick up his next cargo.

During this time Captain Little was gritting his teeth over the major problem. The temptation was to fly to New Caledonia and radio to Colonel Claude ("Sheriff") Larkin at Pearl Harbor that he lacked equipment to do anything on Efate, and if he did that, there was a good chance that Larkin would recall the forward echelon on the same convoy that had carried it out. True, it was painful to think of the disappointment of the British and Aussies who had been praying for an airfield to protect the island. But it was risky business to go ahead with slow work enforced by the lack of tool-power, ever in danger of having the strip spotted by Japanese reconnaissance from the air; and once they had a glimpse of what was in progress, they were sure to strike Efate, and strike in force. Work which should have been done on the run would have to be accomplished at a snail's pace. It would be something like walking across the target on a rifle range. But it is the very essence of the Marine legend that expeditions must always do what they can, no matter how far from support or how badly undermanned. Besides, Little was a builder who'd had to fight to meet deadlines many a time before this. He decided to take the chance. In fact, he had been trying to locate a possible site for the strip from the first. Before the *Crescent City* heaved to off Vila, he had ordered Technical Sergeant Liefke to make a flight in the Duck with the pilot, Sergeant Woolley. Liefke was top photographer for the echelon. The Pearl Harbor attack had knocked him out of his "sack" to photograph the destruction of America's bastion of the Pacific. Now he was deep in the Pacific itself with an order to map the coastline of Efate so that the pictures could be sent back to Hawaii on the *Crescent City*.

That first mission into Efate's sky was a promise of what was to come. Woolley flew up into brilliant sunshine that changed in a few minutes to a sky of rain and thunder. The rain ceased; still there was rolling fog and mist through which Woolley had to tool the plane until pictures were taken. Later the rain came again. Before the day ended, Liefke, with Osimo and Pruitt, his assistants, were laboring over a pile of soaked photographic equipment, their precious supplies, that had been heaped on the dock. They were disgusted, disheartened, and profane, a bitter forecast of what the whole forward echelon was to feel before long. The old wooden printer had collapsed into a sodden mass of warped boards and fungus-covered glass at the first attempt to lift it. All the film, except what was packed in metal containers, was ruined, and that was true of the photographic paper, also. They could rescue only scraps and fragments. But now Liefke went up with Woolley again to try to photograph a suitable site for that airfield which might have to be built. They had to find a spot large enough, flat, not too heavily overgrown.

When finally Little determined to build the strip, he had the developed pictures to help him select a site, but a bird's-eye view of a tropical scene doesn't always tell the naked truth. The captain went out with Liefke to look over the first promising prospect, and for two days there was wading in ankle-deep water plus vain efforts to drain away the flood. It was a coconut plantation that ran to the edge of the ocean, and that would eliminate a good deal of labor in clearing away timber from this end of the strip. Takeoffs could be made over the open sea, and that too seemed good. But now Little remembered the detailed instructions of Lieutenant Colonel Ira L. Kimes about the choice of an airfield site and realized that all this early labor went for nothing. He sat down with Kimes's instructions and rethought the entire problem.

# Jungle Experience

*two*

★ These were the rules as Kimes had laid them down:

1. Explicitly have the camp away from the runways.

2. Keep shops, transportation, and other activities at least five hundred yards away from the field, as the Japs were known to shoot incendiaries at random into the edge of a strip.

3. Have the main camp actually several miles from the runway. Build one-way roads for ingress and egress so that the tropical forest would be more apt to hide the lanes of travel. In every place, maintain "camouflage discipline."

4. Use all the natural cover possible.

5. Blend tents with surrounding country.

6. Build plane revetments away from the runway with camouflaged taxiways to the strip.

All of these rules were reinforced by Captain Little's memories of what had happened to the field at Ewa, on Oahu (Hawaii), when the Japanese bombed it. There had been no plane revetments — protective walls or embankments between which the planes could lie — and there had been no slit trenches, no camouflage, no sandbags to save such valuable communications equipment as radio installations. It had been felt that too many warlike preparations might hurt the feelings of Emperor Hirohito and depress the spirits of the Japanese Peace Party. That was true at Bataan in the Philippines also, but Little wanted to keep his slate clear of error in Efate.

So he cast farther afield and hit at last upon the only piece of ground on the island that was really suitable for his fighter strip and capable of expansion into a bomber runway: a coconut plantation owned by Madame Bladiniere. Madame's heart was so big and her patriotism so perfect that she never complained about the wholesale destruction of her property or attempted to get a price, however small, for her land. So far as is known, she never was compensated for her loss, but she remained throughout a gracious hostess and a comforting friend to the Marines; her pretty daughters were about all that blessed those hungry American eyes. The only return Little could make was to build the strip so that it did not pass through her house or the outbuildings where the copra was prepared.

While the captain conferred with the British and French commissioners about ways and means, Lieutenant Martin was left in charge of the makeshift camp in the paddock. That was when he began to earn his reputation as a "line officer" doctor, taking every responsibility that Little could not assume. And the burden of caring for the troops in camp was enough to break a man's heart.

The first day was typical. They managed to put up a few tents while the rain bucketed down and washed the life out of everything except the tropical flies, which darkened the air as much as the downpour and showed they could bite through even the skin of a Marine. The men had to eat in the open, where the water filled up the coffee cups faster than they drank it. And as the darkness washed up from the horizon in a sudden wave, as it does in that part of the world, the mosquitoes swarmed in by the billions. "They came in to roost. You never saw such birds. You didn't want a fly swatter but a shotgun. They were tired of native meat, and when they found all that American beef, they went to town. They were so damn big you wouldn't think their wings could hold them up. They say up at the Canal [Guadalcanal] there was a plane captain in the dark of the night who got a bit confused and ran fifty gallons of gas into a mosquito before he found out his mistake, but maybe that's exaggerating a little."

After eating and being eaten, the echelon crowded together into the tents, but after a time the water was flooding in, and they spent the night like refugees on a raft.

The kindness of Madame Bladiniere showed them a better site next day, and they went up the side of a mountain to a convenient plateau with a level stretch for the camp and a whole lower world to drain into. The first necessity was a sick bay, and to find lumber for its deck they hunted the town from end to end. A great many of the Marines were running temperatures, and nearly all of them were weakening with diarrhea. It was not due to infected water, flies, and bad food; it was not true dysentery.

"Maybe it's just the change of living in the open, day and night, different air, different humidity and temperature. The nerve system, the whole balance of the body, is adjusted to an environment, and when the environment changes, there is bound to be trouble. I used to go to boys' camp as a kid and found the same thing. Always diarrhea bothering a big percentage of the campers out."

They laid down the deck of the sick bay; they pushed up a galley, gouged out latrines, and waited for the water to drain off the plateau. But it seemed to defy the pull of gravity. The fact was that the water ran from open faucets in the sky, and this torrent kept flooding out the tents. "I think it rained 180 inches during the wetter six months of the year down there, and when the sky was really wringing itself out, the water dropped on us an inch an hour."

The plateau would not do, but there was a knoll still higher up the mountain, and on this the echelon pitched its third and last camp. In the meantime, work on the field had begun, and there was a skinful of weariness added to the troubles of every day. Rate and rank had to be forgotten; the one purpose was to move ground, move it in quantity, and move it fast, for news had come in that was a vital stimulus.

Garlow, the radio brain of the outfit, after heartbreaking days of improvisation and repair of half-ruined apparatus, finally had one receiver going, and the boys at last heard, "This is the United States of America, KFGI, San Francisco." That voice told them that Bataan, our last foothold in the Philippines, finally had fallen. The Japanese were being loosed far and wide across the Pacific, and their nearest American target was the echelon itself. That was one reason why the Marines found the extra strength that kept them at their work, soaking and softening in the rain by days and weeks, then burning raw in the sun, but keeping at it shoulder to shoulder, all those highly specialized crafts subdued to the single purpose.

"Photomen joined with machinist mates, metalsmiths, aerographers, ordnance men, and other skilled technicians. Top-rating master technical sergeants were no better than privates in the mud of Efate, wading in muck and slime above their knees." The food came out of cans, sometimes hot, more often cold. Some days they waded up to the chow-wagon in rain pouring so hard they could not see the fifth man ahead, and got cold beans and baloney. Soaked through and through, they would sit down in the mud and eat with rain streaming down their faces. Or again in

30

the burning sun, sweat-soaked this time, they sat in patches of palm shade with the battered mess kits in their laps, one hand working the spoon while the other waved constantly to keep the flies off.

"The flies were a major part of the horror. They brought with them the smell of the latrines. They would light on a moving hand and had to be brushed off the food. Drinking water came from a sluggish creek below the field, collected in Lister bags and dosed with the foul odor of chlorine. Then night, the damp tents, the wet bedding, the tangle of mosquito netting. If your hand touched the netting while you were asleep, it was covered with welts in the morning."

These were the general conditions of the laborers, and every day their physical stamina grew less and less. They were losing weight fast. There was not a moment of physical comfort. They could not keep from scratching the mosquito bites, and then the broken welts were sure to be infected. Corporal Scroggins, one of the truly devoted spirits in the echelon, showed me twenty great white scars, as big as the end of your thumb, between knee and ankle. They were the result of these infections. The very water in which the boys bathed was thick with a multiplying host of tropical bacteria; every scratch was apt to become infected, and every open infection might turn into a "tropical ulcer," a continuing sore. These grew to full perfection on the native workers. Scratches over their shins — where poor circulation slows up healing processes — bloomed into sickening ulcers three and four inches across, which were treated every day at the sick bay. The same ugly patches kept growing on the Marines.

But now the echelon had been in Efate long enough to develop malaria, and with it began the real troubles of "Line Officer" Doc Martin and his little medical corps. It began in that corps itself when Wright, pharmacist's mate second class, came down with it. "And he still has it. It's chronic with him."

There are two kinds of malaria, the "malignant" and the "benign," though even the "benign" can be a treacherous, close-lurking devil, hard to exterminate. "After the war, malaria of both kinds may break out in many parts of the United States," Martin predicted, "because the germs will be brought back in the blood of returning veterans."

Nearly every member of the echelon became familiar with the three stages of chill, heat, and sweating, with temperatures running up to 105 and 106, though even at such extremes there rarely is delirium. Quinine controls the fever quickly, as a rule, but often the boys could not retain it and had to receive intravenous injections. Besides, they were sadly short of quinine because in the first place they had been posted for Tonga, where malaria is not common. Numbers of the men were at work constantly with the poison accumulating in their bodies; others were knocked flat at a stroke by the malignant form of the disease. The most deadly type is cerebral malaria.

One man came in with a temperature of 102, which did not usually indicate the malignant type, where temperatures ran much higher. He was given quinine at once because he felt very dizzy and was put to bed for regular treatment. At six the next morning Martin was called, because the poor fellow was suddenly in convulsions. Martin had lived in Louisiana, where cerebral malaria was not uncommon, and he luckily recognized the symptoms. The man was in an epileptic type of convulsion, the spine extended, the hands hard-gripped, the tongue protruding so that the teeth have to be wedged open to prevent biting. Two intravenous injections saved this Marine, but it had been a near thing.

What sustained morale throughout was the confidence of the men that Martin would in fact pull them through every crisis. He finally received supplies which enabled him to establish a pro-phylactic routine of two Atabrine treatments weekly, and after that the malaria was kept more in check, though it never was beaten. Medical detail, in the meantime, was left more and more in the competent hands of Chief Pharmacist's Mate Barkowski, so that Martin could give him-self more fully to the main effort: the building of the field.

# Building the Runway

*three*

★ Captain Little was laying out the airfield as best he could. He found a French transit which he set up and went by compass bearing to determine the angles of elevation in order to level the grade of the field. They tied sheets in tall coconut palms to indicate their lines, and bulldozers at once pushed through to make a path around the entire perimeter.

The bulk and nature of the job in this manner were indicated, and the amount of work to be done appalled the captain. If he could not find more engines to labor for him, he must try to secure more pairs of hands. The British commissioner solved that; he moved in six hundred headhunters from a neighboring island. They were black, but not at all like American Negroes. They were short, muscular, stocky, with wild outbushings of hair. They had brilliant teeth and childlike smiles, and "their black skins tossed about the reflections of the sun like mirrors." They never had been fond of the whites they had known before, but they found the Marines a different race and even rubbed their feet raw by pulling Marine shoes onto their earth-hardened calluses.

From French missionaries they had learned a few hymns, but they much preferred "Clementine" and other American songs the Marines taught them. They hungered for American cigarettes too, and altogether they were a faithful, good-natured lot. They never even noticed the weather, because it was the only kind they were used to. They had certain pleasant arts, particularly in cookery, and it was wonderful what they could do when they had a chance to mix a couple of chickens around with wild cabbage, coconuts, and native roots.

These fellows made the "gangs." The Marines had to do the bossing and lend a hand in the hard labor, to keep up the pace. These natives had a way of moving the big palm logs that astonished the Marines. For no matter how big the tree, they would undertake to move it, shoving poles under the trunk and then singing and heaving in time to a chant while the mountain of tree trembled and shuddered and began to creep away by inches. In fact, as long as they could sing, they would do anything and never grow tired. Now that the blacks gave Captain Little hands to work with, he kept them steadily at it. He covered the whole area of the field with stakes to mark the fills and cuts, so that the natives gradually began to learn the system. At first they had not the least idea of what to do with picks and shovels, however. They started filling the shovels by hand.

Eventually there were reasonably efficient groups at work, some cutting trees down and into sections while others burned fallen trees, or carried underbrush and stumps to the sides of the field, or toiled with shovels — such a hardy-looking tribe that they seemed impervious to chills and fever. They were not, however, for the curse of the anopheles seems to fall on all races of all colors with equal virulence. The doctor, short on medical rations for the echelon, was in despair about the condition of the blacks, and once again it was the British commissioner who came to the rescue. He donated nine thousand five-grain quinine ampules, which were like nine thousand second chances at life. By that time some of the poor fellows were too weak to come for medicine, so they were treated in their own shacks where they lived, rainproof under half a yard of thatching.

In an environment which even natives could not endure, the unsolved mystery is how the white man could take so much, so thick, and so long. In part the answer may be that small troubles wear out the spirit but great ones may be a challenge and a stimulus. Furthermore, a lot of these men were technicians who were incapable of surrendering to their problems. There was again the bright example of the two officers, Little and Martin, working harmoniously and selflessly together, day and night, with unfaltering good cheer. Good habits can be learned, and the echelon practiced smiling, even with set teeth.

It was the equipment of the Transportation Department that proved crucial in the building of the field. There were two light Army cargo trucks, a dump truck, a truck crane and trailer, a fire-and-crash truck, a field-lighting truck, a field ambulance, and a panel truck. The two vital hands that tore away the jungle were the bulldozers: an RD8 113-horsepower Caterpillar, and a smaller R4 Caterpillar. They worked behind the dynamite, gouging out earth and trees, leveling what would become an airfield.

When a bit of surface had been leveled, finger coral was laid on for a resistant surface. But the next morning it was discovered that the surface portion was all great humps and bulges — mushrooms which, when kicked, crumbled away to nothing with a puff of the humid air that had raised them. It became clear that the two feet of rich tropical humus could not be considered soil. Every particle of it had to be scraped away to get at the raw, red gum of the clay beneath. The bulldozers were called on to peel off that worthless upper surface as soon as the trees were cleared, chiefly through their work. Staff Sergeant Powers knew exactly how to make a short run with the RD8 and bang into a palm a foot and a half in diameter. His knees were kept black and blue by falling coconuts. When the big palms came out, they left a hole six feet deep and the same width, with a great tangle of roots. Powers had the bad luck to catch the bulldozer's blade on a tree stump and cracked the massive hanger bolt, and after that, in spite of welding, the thing kept on breaking.

Bulldozers are not meant to be used as battering rams, after all, and every now and then a radiator would also be smashed, which meant a twenty-four-hour job for Sergeant Vernie Bledsoe and his right-hand man, Jim Helm, laboring with a borrowed welding torch and scraps of metal picked up here and there. But there never was a good junk pile to pick from on Efate.

Men like Shampel and Perry spent their days lying under trucks in a foot of mud trying to do repairs while the flies blackened their faces and hands. Finally they preferred the quieter and more poisonous hell of mosquitoes at night to the flies during the day; by this time the men were taking for granted the malarial mist before the eyes and aches in the marrow bones.

Their sleeping hours became a torment, because the men on guard were continually shooting at ghosts and rousing the camp. Night in the tropical jungle is not like the calm of darkness of a northern woodland. There is always a stir of life, quiet slitherings and splashings, and now and then pale gleams or sudden up-flashings of phosphorescence, for in the wet heat of the jungle, life is forever building or consuming in quick decay. And nervous patrols, with their minds full of stories of raiding Japanese who walk invisible by night, were continually turning loose a blast at these glimmers of light. Then there were actual prowlers, because many of the plantation laborers were imported Tonkinese who could work all day and wander all night without wearing down, particularly if they felt that a spare tool or even an old shoe could be snitched from the camp. If a patrol grabbed one of these Tonkinese, the fellow would roll his eyes and understand nothing; but they looked like hunting cats and gave the guards a lot of trouble. So it was quite a time before the shooting at ghosts and Tonkinese by night ended and the echelon could have all the sleep the mosquitoes permitted. Under these conditions the building of the field went forward in a nightmare of effort and illness, but now that the jungle was melting away from the strip, the men carried on with more cheerfulness, because they could see the goal in outline like a face in a mist, and soldiers don't mind fighting if they have a chance to win.

The field itself was almost less labor than the maintenance of the roads that led to it. For the sake of camouflage, these roadways had to be winding trails, which from the sky would show no break in the forest green. The little eight-foot paths could not be properly graded for drainage, and the result was that transport was a miserable amphibious operation. "Some of those roads, the trucks would sink in above their wheels. There was a tractor once that kept on going down till all we could see was the exhaust pipe. We had a hell of a lot of grief in there. Nearly every time the problem had a new face, a damned ugly face, and we'd stand around and scratch our heads and try to think of a solution. Somebody would get an idea, and it wasn't always the officers or the noncoms, because the privates were right in there using gray matter as well as the strength of their backs. Finally along would come a bulldozer and begin to carve the muck away so that we could make another rescue."

Of course, such muck would not do as a surface for the strip. They had to truck in sand, and it was the worst, most uneven sand in the world, continually developing soft spots that had to be cut out and replaced; and the surface of it either was slicing away in the rain or else blowing off in clouds when a dry spell came. So finger coral was again brought in, and with it the top dressing of the field was completed.

All this inching progress was accomplished by men who were undernourished. They were on a hideous routine of Vienna sausage, corned beef, Vienna sausage, canned tongue, Vienna sausage, canned salmon, Vienna sausage. . . . Scheinost was the mess sergeant. "I felt for those boys, but I had to give 'em the only food that was at hand, and I used to say, when they'd yell at me, 'Wait till I slip half a coconut on your plate and say here it is. Don't howl till then!' " Coffee was made in GI garbage cans that held about forty gallons. "I'd fill the can with water, bring it to a boil, throw in the grounds, and let it keep on boiling until it was strong enough. It wasn't so bad when it was first made, but after an hour it used to turn green in the can. Still, the boys would come back for seconds." They were having too

40

much taken out of them every day, and they had to have something to replace it. "Even that green filth was something because it was hot, and we *called* it coffee."

The food hardest to stomach was the dehydrated potatoes. The American is a potato-eating mammal, but the dehydrated potato is a sad sight. Mixed with water, it looks like wallpaper paste and tastes about the same. "We boiled and we mashed and we fried them, but the boys never liked the stuff. There was nothing to do but try to fix up a gravy so good that the boys couldn't taste the potatoes, but we didn't have the ingredients to make the gravy most of the time. I've had fellows come to me doggone near crying, but what are you gonna do?

"We used to go out and float dynamite over the shallows that were full of fish," Sergeant Scheinost continued, "and when the dynamite exploded, it left the fish stunned for a while. Then we'd start after them with two types of spears made by Helm and Bledsoe, who could make anything. One type was a bundle of prongs made of wire or welding rod. Another was a barbed prong on the end of a rod as big as your finger. We got some fish that were fine eating. There were parrotfish with beaks like their name and a kind of wise, angry look on their faces. Somebody said they fed on coral, but how can a fish live on rock? They were red and green and blue, all mixed, the most beautiful colors you ever saw. There were other fish too, so damn pretty it was a shame to eat them."

But even with the fish to piece out the diet from time to time, the forward echelon remained insatiably hungry, and something had to be done about it. Various things *were* done, nearly all unofficial, but Scheinost was a veteran and so was Barkowski of the Medical Department. These two lived together in a grass shack that made some of the pleasantest history on Efate, and they put their brains together to see how they could get food out of the far larger and better-supplied Army camp. They needed a key to those supplies, a wet key. So somehow they got hold of 180-proof alcohol, which they combined with cherry juice, lemon or orange powder, glycerine, and water. They needed the glycerine in that drink to slide it down a-ways, because a Marine doesn't mind what happens to his deeper vitals, but he hates to lose the lining of his mouth and throat. A few drinks of this mixture applied to the proper personnel caused various gates to open, and whole truckloads of food were carted off to the starving echelon.

# Captain Little's Crisis

*four*

★ It wasn't all misery. There was the day of the Great Barbecue, for instance. Before this great occasion, a cow had been bought from Madame Bladiniere and staked out with a sign on it to signify that this bit of beef was to die for a good cause on such and such a day, and the morale of the whole echelon picked up amazingly in expectation.

Helm and Bledsoe, who could do anything, proved it again by blasting out a barbecue pit, and from the creek large rocks were carried. Chick Hagstrom, his baby face shining like a harvest moon, made the barbecue sauce. "What I mean is, it *was* a sauce. Ginger root, tabasco sauce, ketchup, Worcestershire, canned tomatoes, garlic, celery salt, pepper, and hot peppers — you pick them wild in the jungle, and hot is hot. That ginger is the best flavoring you ever had in your life. Maybe the Chinese might have it, and in the States, but nobody else. Got a skin like a potato; looks something like a horseradish root, but all curled up. You only take a couple of slices."

Furthermore: "We had a salad that was prime.

The bulldozers had picked it for us by knocking down palm trees, and inside the tree, where the leaves all fall out, there is 'heart of palm salad.' It's a choice bit; it resembles an elephant tusk, nice and pointed. You kill the tree when you get it out, and you don't ordinarily grow a tree twenty-five years for the sake of one salad, but it's almost worthwhile. Then we had a root called tara, like sweet potatoes, only we liked them better. (Mind you, when the boys got their first raw Irish potatoes later on, they walked around eating them like apples.) We baked those tara roots with oleomargarine, and the boys yelled for more. There were other roots called tapioca, shaped like French bread, and we sliced them up and put them on the griddle and fried them and seasoned them up till they were just like a potato cake. And by golly, were they good! You'd be surprised. We had beer, we had corn. The ears of corn, it isn't believable, they were eighteen inches long and three inches in diameter. The cucumbers looked like watermelons. The ordinary seed from the United States just builds up like that when it gets a chance to live in a Turkish bath for nothing. One slice you'd have to cut into quarters; from six of them with onions you could feed two hundred men. That country down there, you put a stick in the ground, and the doggone thing would sprout. We built a fence, and in a week it came alive. The shack I had started to turn green and lift itself. Dead bamboo would sprout, and you know how dead bamboo is."

Getting back to the Great Party: "Madame Bladiniere and everybody was there. We got the headhunters of Malakula that had been working on the field to come down and put on a powwow. They dance right up and down in one place, and they pounded the earth down ten inches with their heels. The singing was full of harmony, like a lovely chant, and they stomp and stomp and keep on beating the ground down into a regular trough. We'd slipped them some beer to get them in the mood, but they certainly rounded the party off. And after they finished with us, they went over to Madame Bladiniere's and danced the rest of the night, because once they got their feet started, they just couldn't leave off."

Anyone who wanted an exciting game of poker dropped in at the famous shack of Scheinost and Barkowski. The shack was twenty by twenty with a deck of split palm, and the two bedrooms were screened with muslin and mosquito netting. The living room was decorated too, with Varga pictures out of *Esquire* and "the World's Most Beautiful Girls," and "there wasn't any kind of girl you wanted that you couldn't find somewhere on that wall." In fact, not only was the shack considered charming, but the two old-line sergeants had used their brains to equip it with modern comfort and convenience. There was a kerosene icebox that held fifteen quarts and turned out plenty of ice cubes, but the high point of equipment was a ten-dollar phonograph that they bought for a mere seventy-five along with some

45

records no more than three years old. "You'd listen to the damn things and it was funny, the next you knew, your eyes would start getting wet." Besides all this, Barkowski had been given by a missionary a complete skull of a chief of one of the headhunter tribes. Coconut husk mixed with mud was the plastic with which the features had been restored on the skull. "It was forty years old, and Barkowski named it Oscar." When Scheinost saw it for the first time, Barkowski was sitting beside the table having a drink, and on the other side of the table, keeping him company, was Oscar with a fuming cigar in his mouth and a couple of machetes crossed under his chin. Scheinost moved out for the night.

But the main business of the shack was to house the poker game. It cost Barkowski a hundred dollars to sit in at the opening session, and after that he was the audience. "Scheinost made a Christian of me," said Barkowski ruefully. "He made a Christian of everybody, including Martin and Ross and Davis. Ross is a real beany guy and a deep thinker, but he never could dig as deep as Scheinost. Nobody ever could."

This master craftsman at poker, unlike most of the real technicians, talks freely about his art, and he's worth hearing.

"There's only one way of playing cards. I'll tell you the truth, I've never done anything in my life that I'm really ashamed of, but love, war, and cards are all about the same. I don't dislike draw poker, but stud is better for me. The main thing

46

is, don't ever run. You deal them out and start shuffling and fumbling around, but you keep your mind working. He has an ace in the hole, and your own layout is pretty weak, but don't run. You check on him, and you start shelling out, and you stay in to see the last card. When a guy is bluffing, I'll buck him till hell won't hold him. I learned the hard way. For seventeen years everything I earned went for poker. Then it came to me, the way you learn a foreign language. One day you're dumb, the next day you can talk. It came to me like that. I played without mercy, but straight. Something crooked, I'd throw in my cards and quit. And the final thing is, don't play poker unless you like it the way Will Rogers liked chicken.[1] He'd take a piece in his hand and growl over it."

Barkowski added to this, solemnly: "Over there in Shanghai, Will Rogers ate one night in the officers' mess and the next night with the mess of the pharmacist's mates. He came in and ordered a quart of sherry for every man, and we all sat there, him included, and we each drank that one quart of sherry wine with the meal. And he was the greatest goddamn man I ever saw in my life."

Captain Little gradually had been accumulating the malarial poison, for the mosquito netting was only a partial protection, and if in the night a man's hand or leg touched the netting, he could count twenty or thirty welts on the skin next

47

morning. As for the men in Transportation, working all night long on repairs so that the labor on the field could continue in the day, they were eaten away by the disease. Illness and the responsibility of the field construction, together with the necessity of setting an example to maintain morale, made a triple burden for Little. He could not fight his exhaustion by permitting himself a special diet. He and Doc Martin always ate last, after the men and on the same rations. Coffee and hardtack was the breakfast which had to see them through from the crack of dawn to noon, and it was a steadying influence on the men to know that their commanders suffered through exactly the same conditions as themselves. The weight of a typical day finally cracked Captain Little.

He'd had a hotter touch of fever the afternoon before and went in to spend the night with Stan Jones, the representative of Phipps, Jones, a South Sea trading company with a post at Vila. Jones knew the "bush," the beach, and the sea, and there was nothing he would not do for the Americans. He put Little in the hands of his number one boy, Morris, and Morris doped Little with native medicine plus quinine and steamed him out with a hot bath. But the captain would not spend the time in bed that Morris and Jones advised. He kept in mind that his most urgent purpose was to lead his men in person, not give orders from a distance, so he was up at four in the morning and off for the "swamp," as the natives called the airfield.

There were eight miles to cover, the last three through the gumbo of the churned jungle. Even with heavy chains wrapped around the wheels it was almost impossible to get on, for the wheels kept sinking through the top of the grade, and the decayed tropical humus was more grease than clay. It was always discouraging work, that lurching, straining labor through the muck, but this morning it sickened the captain. And the rain was a waterfall thundering on the top of the "panel wagon" he drove. For twenty-nine days there had been rain with few intermissions, rain so thick it made a sensible burden on the shoulders of a man walking through it, rain that washed away the air needed for breathing. "A fish could live in that kind of an atmosphere," said Little, "but a man?" However, he won through to the field.

He was on time too, for the natives arrived at 5:45 to begin their day's work. They were already a sickly lot and full of homesickness for their own islands. But Sergeant Major Ross was there as usual with his peculiar talent for handling them. They called him Master, and he knew how to rally their spirits for another day's effort. Besides, they were getting medical attention, and Little's principle was "If we work them, we take care of them." It was not all rain on this particular morning of disaster. Little remembered the tropical birds doing their bright best, so beautiful that he didn't try to describe them but sat and smiled at the memory; the jungle was blooming like fire, and the cocoa trees kept a sweetness in the air. But none of that loveliness was worth a damn, because the big bulldozer, the one efficient tool for knocking over the palm trees, had broken down again, this time hopelessly smashed, it seemed. The transport men grimly assured the captain that they would have it working within a day, but as he looked at the smashed radiator, the heart went out of him. He should have cheered them on with the right words, but all at once he felt like a liar who had told his last lie. There was no use pretending.

He drove on toward the camp. "There was some tropical fruit that had dropped off the trees, dead ripe. Dead was the way it smelled, too. And it seemed to me like the wrong part of the world for me to be in. I had to get out of the truck and vomit. I can still smell that stench of ripe fruit if I half try." He got back in the truck and drove on, reached the sick bay through a sort of haze, and found Martin there. "I felt mighty sorry for Doc, the way he'd been a doctor, line officer, and friend to all of us. I felt sorry for all the forward echelon, and I was able to see their faces — all through rain, dimly, Ross, and Jenkins, and Griffis, and DeBenedictis, and the whole echelon that had been pouring out its heart to do the work that I'd been fool enough to plan for them. I could see them, and I could see that the job would never be done.

" 'Doc, we're licked,' I said. 'We can't build an airstrip in a swamp with broken equipment and sick men. I'm sending a dispatch to Pearl Harbor that we can't make it.'

" 'All right,' said Doc. 'You can do that tomorrow. Today you're going to bed.'

"It was a comforting thing to have somebody give me an order. My knees were weak. I was weak in the head, too. I couldn't face up to anything more. So I went to bed, but Doc didn't pass the bad word down the line. Nobody knew what I had in mind. He turned himself into two men and kept the sick bay going and ran things on the strip at the same time, until the sickness cleared away from me and I was able to see a spot of hope again." That was why the fighter strip finally was completed by the echelon. "Martin was the wheel horse, and when I lay down, he pulled the whole load and me along with it."

# First Planes Land on the Strip

*five*

★ All this time the fear of the Japs kept the men looking into the north, and there was reason to expect that trouble might drop on them out of the skies or rise at them from the sea at any moment. Jap planes actually reconnoitered Efate, and submarines stuck up their periscopes to look at the shore, but camouflage and the sage advice of Kimes prevented the enemy from seeing what was happening on the island. And the same rain that kept the echelon cursing was also a mist in the eyes of Japanese observers.

It was no longer technically the Forward Echelon of Group 24. It had been assigned as the ground force of Heavier-Than-Air Marine Fighter Squadron 212 (VMF-212) under the command of Major, soon to be Lieutenant Colonel, Harold W. Bauer, who was to come down from Hawaii eventually with the planes and pilots that would give the organization teeth to fight with. It was cheering news, because Bauer was a known man. But still there were anxious days before he arrived to take over command.

News kept coming from the Royal Australian Air Force secret base on Efate, where the big

PBYs were fueled for reconnaissance over Rabaul, Salamaua, and Lae, and over Guadalcanal with its listening posts and shortwave radios, which kept feeding news of the Japanese to the Efate base.[1] The Australians on Guadalcanal were in small force, but rarely have such small numbers done more effective duty, tickling the very chin whiskers of the Jap Navy and Air Force. In order to make their occupation troops seem more formidable, they kept changing camp and letting their laundry be seen in new positions, so that the Japs might feel that the island was fairly bristling with enemies, and so delay their attack until they had organized a real armada. The Australians had a lucky break when a Jap patrol bomber, taking a low look at the terrain, was struck by .30-caliber bullets from a machine-gun nest and brought down by a lucky burst. After that, the Japs presumed that Guadalcanal was dangerous indeed, and they never again flew low over the land.

The news which was transmitted from the radios on Guadalcanal was picked up and interpreted on Efate by Flight Officer W. O. Sands, an ex–airline pilot in Australia. During his days as a commercial aviator he had flown over New Guinea and others of the important islands, and he had the rare gift of the true strategist who knows how to guess at large operations from the merest straws that blow in the wind. All his predictions came true. As early as April 1942 he was predicting that the Japs would make a great effort to take Port Moresby in New Guinea and thence push on south to establish bases in the New Hebrides. His thinking gave hope to Little and Martin; they studied his big map and began to share his belief that Efate might be reasonably safe until Moresby fell.

But bad news kept slapping the face of Captain Little. There was one grim official report that the Japs had attacked Samoa, and Efate stood by for invasion by air the next morning. Nothing came out of that except nerves stretched tighter than drumheads. But later there was word of the enemy dropping down from Truk,[2] and that was not just fancy. They were in force; they had big ideas; they were slamming toward Port Moresby and the New Hebrides, said Flight Officer Sands. And there was no doubt that he was right. The critical stage — the first great critical stage — of the battle of the South Pacific was beginning.

To the men on Efate it seemed madness to keep on muddling in that overheated greenhouse while the fate of things was being worked out just to the north and disaster was so certain to slip south onto their heads. The certainty of defeat sprang out of the unending series of Jap victories. Six months before, the Japs had come out of the dark to do their treachery and murder at Pearl Harbor, and ever since they had been expanding over the Pacific like a nova in the sky, rushing from one success to another. They had the impetus of victory that dazes the brain of the loser and strengthens the heart of the winner. But then incredibly glorious news came in as a promise, a hint, and then as a settled fact. One of the great sea battles had taken place in the Coral Sea, to the west of Efate, on May 8, and the Japs no longer could say that the Son of Heaven always was victorious; his invasion of Port Moresby and perhaps of Australia had been turned back, and he had lost two aircraft carriers.[3] Above all, he had not remained to win or die. His remaining ships had run for their lives.

That was the first great mercy for the men on Efate. After that, even the rains let up a little. A closer organization and more familiarity with the work let the construction of the field progress even more rapidly, in spite of the weakness caused by the malaria and the bad food. Under Sergeant Ross there were Garner, Coyle, and Greenhagen to give three subheads to the toilers. Among the cooks, Corporal Heath had developed a line of chatter that kept the men laughing even while they consumed the daily curse of dehydrated potatoes.

Then they had their first great day, the first justification of all the labor they had put in. An SNJ (a two-seated trainer) and three SBDs (dive bombers) came in and effected safe landings on the strip. The ground force of VMF-212 stood by and yelled, though this was not the ultimate test. Both of these types of planes had reasonably low landing speeds; fighter planes would come in much faster. Yet the first test had been passed.

Word now came that Bauer and the fighter pilots were coming in, and the next day Bauer arrived in a Catalina PBY-5A Flying Boat to examine the field before sending in his pilots and to have his first glimpse of the other half, the ground-crew portion, of his squadron.

There was only a chance for brief impressions of a tall two-hundred-pounder with the quick, alert ways of a little man. After graduating from Annapolis, where he starred in football and other sports and later returned to join the coaching staff, Bauer had spent seven years in Marine aviation. He was a native of the Kansas-Nebraska plains and at the Naval Academy had been given the nickname Indian Joe because of his dark complexion, high cheekbones, and prominent jaw. His true name was Harold William Bauer, but he was always Joe to family and friends. His pilots were already referring to him as the Coach, because he treated them like members of a team, taught them much, and, at thirty-four, was a decade older than many of them.

He seemed to members of the crew astonishingly cheerful, not with the good nature of a vacuous mind, but with the zest of a fellow who expects to find that there is fun and a game in war itself. He saw Martin and Little and went silently over the field of their labor. Before he had finished his survey, he noticed their battered, much-welded equipment, also, and he knew what the true nature of their work had been. He told them what he thought of the job they had done, and what he thought of them for doing it, speaking with that direct and almost impatient eagerness that made other men feel his sincerity.

Then he was away in the Catalina, leaving behind him a strong sense that all they had heard about him was true and also less than the truth. He had said enough to make them feel rewarded for what they had done, and every day thereafter he kept holding up the building of that fighter strip as one of the bright events of the whole war. They knew he would be that way. "He was that sort of a man, with the extra passion of faith in the people under his command." Bauer had confirmed the fact as reported to him that the unfinished field was too short for landing fighter planes. This was the reason why he and his fighters, approaching by aircraft carrier, had been obliged to fly nearly four hundred miles further to New Caledonia to begin their intensive training and wait while the Efate field was lengthened that vital bit.

Bauer had come to the echelon like sun after rain, but more trouble was gathering in the north and more intimately close to Efate. Though turned away from Port Moresby, the Japs had occupied Guadalcanal. The Aussies there were never more than a force for demonstration. In the language of Sergeant Scheinost, they had been playing a bluff as though it were a real hand, with the result that they delayed the Japanese occupation for vital weeks and weeks — during which that invaluable airfield from which they were to be struck and wounded, again and again, was developing on Efate — but now the Japanese descended in an irresistible wave on Guadalcanal. The Aussies had to get out, and get out fast. "But they left one man behind them. He volunteered to stay. His name was McFarland, I think. And all the time the Japs were there, McFarland stuck in the Guadalcanal jungle and spied them out. Think of staying there alone — think of even thinking of doing it! But he got the word away on his radio, and that was why we knew so well where Henderson Field, as it would be called, was located, and how it progressed as the Japs built it. That was why our bombers weren't hitting in the dark when the time came. I would have liked to see this McFarland. I wouldn't mind going all the way down to Australia, after this man's war, to shake hands with him."

# Green Pilots Train at New Caledonia

## six

★ That flight from the carriers *Enterprise* and *Hornet* to Tontouta on New Caledonia, as an interim step toward Efate, was something the half-fledged pilots of 212 were not to forget. They'd been twelve days at sea from Hawaii, eager to get off the deck, but now it was soupy, dirty weather. It was also their first flight off a carrier, and their navigation skills were not by any means perfect. But Bauer led them four hundred miles through the dark of that sky and put them all down safely except Major Quilter. Hardly a plane among the twenty-one had more than a gallon of gas left when they reached Tontouta, and Quilter, running completely out while he was still over water, had to ditch in the sea just off-shore, but he was brought in safely.

It was May 10, 1942, and for a month Bauer poured the training into them, rain or shine, 625 hours in twenty-eight days. The island was not such a wet green hell as Efate. They could get out deer hunting now and then, and the venison was delicious, particularly when there was wine to serve with it. There were goats to shoot in the hills too, but never enough hunting chances to change the diet very much, so that the chief complaint was the one which kept rising from the South Pacific in those days like a groan. Soggy pancakes every morning, and chili hash and dehydrated potatoes the rest of the day. "You sit down hungry, and you eat till you're full, and still you're hungry." It was bad enough for the ground crew; it was twenty times worse for the pilots who had to get up there to high altitude where they used their oxygen masks, and oxygen burns a man out, consumes the very marrow in his bones, so he needs meat, lots of it. Instead they got dehydrated potatoes. They grew thin. But Bauer kept them whirling in a three-ring circus in the sky, and they were so keen to learn out of his book that they tended to overlook everything else. Besides, they were just getting to know one another, and that knowledge would be as important as it is to a football team, except that in this game the fellow who played beside you made the difference between living and dying.

These boys already had been schooled in the usual acrobatics, with slower planes. They could do Immelmanns, snap rolls, wingovers, cartwheels, slow rolls, and the rest of the gymnastics which actually in battle tactics are rarely used; but "to keep one's hand in, one goes up and wrings them out, because the acrobatics give you the feel of your plane in different positions." They had learned to land on hundred-foot circles. They had practiced cut-gun landings, mortally important if an engine fails in the takeoff before there is much altitude. "The thing to do is to nose over and make a good landing instead of stalling out, but the normal reaction is to haul right back on the stick and try to land immediately, but you haven't enough air speed and control to do that, and it's usually disastrous." Back in the States they had done regular pylon work, flipper turns, formation flying, and they had flown on regular airway beams. They had done the latter blind, to learn once and forever that instruments don't lie to you — very often.

They had backgrounds of flying in which they had learned these things and others. A few, like Everton and Payne, were veterans of the air, but the rest found their new Grumman Wildcats to be pretty hot numbers, and they had to practice all maneuvers with care. The Grumman F4F-3 Wildcat was a stubby, compact affair with a personality of its own. "It looked mean — reminded me of my bull terrier that growled a bit even when his boss went by." Like all planes meant for landings on the deck of a carrier, it had been strengthened to endure the heavy shock, and the strengthening meant the addition of much otherwise unnecessary weight. The result was that it lacked speed and acceleration and high maneuverability. On the other hand, it was durable and well armored, and it carried four of the .50-caliber machine guns — on Guadalcanal the F4F-4s would carry six — whose converging streams of fire were to tear to pieces so many Zeros and Jap bombers. It could take a beating and give one, and upon this pair of facts Bauer built his tactics.

In the early days of the war, knowing that the Zero, the Japs' main fighter, could fly rings around its American counterparts, our system was to hang up in the sun, make a good pass at the Jap, and then go home. But Bauer changed all that. His idea was to capitalize on the fact that the Zero lacked armor and heavy firepower. It had been stripped of weight in order to gain maneuverability, climb, and speed, but it had been lightened to the point of vulnerability. Bauer was the first to teach the value of closing with a Zero and then hanging on to it like a bulldog, turning into it head-on no matter how it flipped around in the air. In the ring, you could call him an exponent of infighting.

In order to prepare his men for this dangerous business, Bauer not only taught them flying tactics that could be used in dogfights; he dwelt on gunnery, gunnery, gunnery from dawn to dark. When there was not a "sleeve" to shoot at, he had the boys make passes on a target plane. "It takes a great deal of practice to make a smooth pass, steadily, with the ball staying right in the center of the turn-and-bank indicator that shows there is neither skidding nor slipping. And to be any good, a man has to have the ball right there. It means you're not swinging your nose from one side to the other and that you're not in a skid."

The best gunnery practice was on the tubular sleeve, which was two feet in diameter and eighteen feet long, towed on a three-hundred-foot cable, and if a man could plaster the sleeve regularly while making his passes, he was reasonably sure to do pretty well against an enemy plane. The passes that Bauer taught were the beam, the high side, and above all the overhead.

Major Ross Jordan, veteran Marine pilot risen through the ranks, stated, "Either Bauer invented the overhead pass, or else he was the first to show what really could be done with it. Before the war, he used to do some funny flying in target practice, and he put so many shots into the sleeve that nobody could believe it. They suspected he was using extra ammunition, but when they gave his ammunition a close check, they found he was still getting the same results. After that, they were willing to listen to what he said about gunnery."

The overhead pass looks both complicated and absurd. In it the flyer approaches his enemy head-on from a superior altitude. At the right moment he turns over on his back, so as to keep the other plane in view, and then dives on the target, so that his speed is being at least in part subtracted from the speed of the enemy plane, and this maneuver gives a chance for a prolonged burst. It seems like crazy gymnastics; actually it is rather like the swinging of a golf club with a long follow-through. "The overhead pass was Greek to the Zeros. It wasn't in the books. The trouble with it was that the Zero flew so much better than the Grumman that some of our pilots never found themselves above a Jap."

63

Bastian, one of the smoothest flyers of 212, summed up the major features of the Bauer system as follows:

1. Get altitude on the other fellow if you can.
2. Try to use surprise, by coming out of the sun or a cloud.
3. Be on the alert with your eyes. Trouble may be coming from either side, above, or below, so keep your head mounted on a swivel. Remember that absolutely nothing can be heard over the roar of the motor except your radio earphones; the eyes have to tell you everything else. To look directly below, drop your wing.
4. When he has the jump on you by being above you, the best thing you can do is to keep him off your tail, where he's going to try to be. So keep below if you have to, but at any rate stay behind him. This is hard, because extra altitude can be turned into speed at any moment, and speed can mean quick maneuvers; but try to bring your guns to bear on him whenever he brings his to bear on you.
5. As he turns into you, you are turning into him, keeping your head to him. You can't outclimb him in this way unless you're very careful, but you're apt to hurt him as much as he hurts you. This system of turning up against each pass of the enemy is called scissoring.
6. In scissoring, the Jap, being in a faster and more maneuverable plane, ought to be able to work out of the scissors and get on your tail.

So you simply have to outthink him a bit.

7. In this business you have to guess one move ahead. If you guess wrong, you may be brushed right out of the sky. But the Jap is not inventive or resourceful in the air. Once you learn his pattern of flying, you can be fairly sure that he will stick to the same system of maneuvers. Then you can take liberties and cut a few corners.

These were the essentials of the Bauer system, by no means as simple as it may sound, because the final feature of it is that the underdog must fly better than the man on top. In other words, Bauer's idea was good for a fine air tactician with the teeth of a wolf and the wits of a fox, but it was an easy way to die for a fellow who didn't know the fine points.

That was what the colonel taught his men: the fine points. Over and over again he was up in the air practicing dogfights with them, offering a dollar to any man who could get on the tail of his plane. "He'd go up in a slower SNJ trainer and so outmaneuver the pilot in the far superior Grumman that the guy came down despondent. And after a bit of verbal explanation, Bauer would take him up with him and put on the same show against another Grumman. He would give altitude to the other fellow and show the wards and parries against that advantage."

Bauer's football background helped in the charting of these air plays, as anyone can understand who has seen a team at blackboard practice. At Annapolis, on service teams as player and, afterwards, coach, he had been best brain and triple-threat star on every squad. Though never a very fast man, he knew how to be at the right place at the right time. They say he was always breaking out into the open by doing the unexpected, but what seemed improvised on the spot had been charted and planned long before. Bauer was a star for the Navy team that beat Army at Miami, 12–0. And always, big as he was, it was the brainwork that counted, the shifts of tactics, the quick sense of the other fellow's weakness, the sudden device that blocked against his strength. In the air he simply made his squadron his team and instilled in it that selfless devotion to the game which makes men love their work and one another. He turned sport into war, and he turned war into sport.

He had a great sense of fun, Sergeant Ackerman recalled. "Getting time off one day, Joe Allen and I decided to go to 'town,' where there was a corrugated metal building, the contents of which resembled that of a general store. While Joe and I were looking through the merchandise, we found a couple of old tuxedos, probably made prior to World War I. We purchased these tuxedos, went back to camp, and spent the balance of the afternoon cleaning them up and pressing them. For dinner, he and I decided to wear our tuxedos to the mess hall. There we were, strolling up this dirt road, with our mess gear in hand, headed for our chow. About a hundred yards up the road, we noted Colonel Bauer coming toward us. As he approached I thought to myself, 'Oh, oh! We're in trouble!' However, as the colonel came abreast of us he looked at us and said, 'Good evening, men!' and continued on his way, as if it was the most normal thing in the world to see two of his Marines wearing tuxedos in a jungle in the South Pacific. He was quite a man!

"On another occasion, about eight of us were assigned to dig a drainage ditch alongside the dirt road that ran from the airfield to our living area. As usual, the weather was hot and humid. We were stripped down to our pants, otherwise naked, digging this ditch. We had a sergeant in charge of the detail named Elias. As we were digging and sweating, we noted that Colonel Bauer had landed, in his Wildcat, and a few moments later was walking up the road where we were digging. As he approached, he stopped and watched us for a few moments. Then he said, 'By golly! I need a workout!' He then shed his shirt, flight jacket, and so forth, and jumped into the ditch with us. Grabbing a shovel, away he went! Sergeant Elias watched this for a few minutes and decided, 'If the colonel can do this, then I can, too!' He then jumped into the pit with us. The colonel probably worked in there thirty to forty-five minutes and raised a good sweat. He then got out of the trench, grabbed his gear, and took off toward the living area.

"My memory of the Good Colonel on the airstrip is something else which hasn't faded. Seeing him getting into his F4 Wildcat, one got the impression that he was 'wearing' the aircraft! He was such a large man! Also, as his record indicated, he flew with great skill and dexterity."

One unhappy blow fell on the squadron before the training at Tontouta ended. Among the pilots was Second Lieutenant Arthur Finucane of Pasadena, California, a tall, slender, fine-looking fellow, very popular with the other pilots. Out in the harbor there was at this time a derelict ship hung up on a reef, a perfect target for strafing or bombing, and Finucane was at practice dive-bombing it half an hour before dusk. It was a clear evening, just coming into the quiet time of the day, when Finucane got his altitude, tipped over, and made a perfect dive. It was perhaps too perfect. No one could tell what happened, but it seemed certain that Finucane must have blacked out or had target fixation. Nothing perceptible seemed to be wrong with his plane, but he finished his dive by going straight in, and his body was never found.

"You always think, after a fellow is gone, that there was something special about him. We hadn't been together long enough for me to know him very well, but he was the right kind, and it hurt all of us — the skipper most of all. We had guessed that he was fond of his flyers, but we didn't know how much until we lost Finucane. It was the first time Bauer had to see one of 212 go, and he took it hard and deep."

They held a service for Finucane at the end of the runway at Tontouta with an Army chaplain presiding, and then they made themselves forget. If they let themselves go, thinking about what happened, it spoiled their flying. If a man went in, they simply had to X him out of their minds, the way you lose a piece in chess and the game must go on with what is left, even if it's a castle or a knight that's been taken away.

# The Men That Make a Fighter Squadron

## seven

★ Perhaps it is better to back-track a little and tell something of the way in which the Bauer brain worked when he was picking out men for his squadron at Ewa Field in the Hawaiian Islands. What strikes one at once is that he cared little for the written records of a young flyer but preferred to see with his own eyes, like a horse trainer who studies confirmation more than bloodlines.

There is the case of Lieutenant John F. A. Rogers, for instance, who seemed to do everything possible to give himself a black eye. Rogers had gone to Notre Dame, a school which doesn't soften a boy particularly, but he was never in a plane until December 1940. When he was assigned to Bauer's squadron at Ewa, he had two crack-ups in two days, and that should have been enough to black him out, as far as a commanding officer was concerned.

One morning at ten o'clock of a good clear day, he was sent up on a familiarization hop, just to get the feel of his plane, and started circling the field at two thousand feet. He had four gas tanks,

70

two main ones and two in the wings, and the idea was to use the gas first out of the wing tanks, which were not self-sealing. When he tried to make the switch after takeoff from the reserve tank to the normal cruising tank, the selector valve wouldn't work. It wouldn't take fuel from any of the other tanks, either. Rogers realized that he was too far from the field to get back to it on a glide. When he looked beneath him, he saw nothing but sugarcane fields, which are a bad place to land because of the overwhelming fire hazard. "And because of the stuff they spray on the cane, if you scratch yourself," said Rogers, "you have a fine chance to pick up arsenic poisoning, so I've heard." At any rate, he decided to make a water landing. He hit the sea and went down in less than two minutes.

"There was a lot of Army to see me going down, but maneuvers were going on, and perhaps they thought I was part of the show. That's the way the Army brain works. They do the best they can, but God help the Marines. I finally managed to peel off my headgear and parachute so that I could swim to shore. I'd hit my head on the gunsight and opened up a pretty bad cut. They could see some blood, so they got me to a doctor, but Army doctors only use the left lobe of the brain, believe me. This fellow thought that I was crazy. He kept saying, 'What day is it? Who is president?' I watched the blood drip and didn't say anything, but I kept thanking God that I was in the Marines. Finally a Navy doctor got to me, and everything was different. They have some brains in the Navy, because they are connected with the Marines, I suppose. They let me ride up forward with the doctor because I was sure that I'd conk out if I had to lie flat on the stretcher. Afterwards he took four or five stitches in my scalp and did such a good job that you need a magnifying glass now to see where he worked."

This was not exactly the sort of flying, or flying luck, that commends a twenty-two-year-old aviator to a crack commanding officer. Rogers went right on to pile misery on misery. Bauer was having his boys land on the Schofield Barracks golf course where two fairways adjoined. Rogers was the last man in his flight, and due to his misunderstanding of his section leader's directions, he grew confused about the landing and had to circle the field again. By the time he was finishing his circuit, all the rest of the planes in the flight had landed and were down at one end of the field. He tried to land on the last half of the field where there was a double-tracked road, perhaps used by the greenskeeper. Again he exercised poor judgment, lacked landing space, ran into the stump of a tree, and tore a wheel off. He almost wished it had been his head.

"I was mad, and I was sick, too. I could imagine what an ace like Bauer thought about a dumb bunny like me, and I didn't want him to have to waste his breath speaking his mind. So I went in to see him and said that if I couldn't fly any better than that, there was no point in my staying with the squadron. I even pulled off my wings, but he wouldn't take them. He said, 'Sit down, Rogers.'

"I sat down. I'd hoped that I could avoid hearing what he would need to say, but I saw that it was my time to burn, so I set my teeth and got ready to take it. But he said, 'I've been flying in the Marine Corps for a long time. I've seen a lot of crack-ups, and I've had a couple myself. I don't think I was a poor flyer then, but perhaps I'm a better flyer now because the bad luck helped me to build up better judgment. You're staying with me. Put on those wings again.' So I put on the wings."

The case of Larry Faulkner ("Cloudy," to 212) is an even clearer proof that Bauer was more interested in men than in performances — men as he knew them rather than men as they had been. Faulkner had been at Midway Island under command of Colonel William Wallace. He was flying a dive bomber, and in landing he ran off the runway through some tar barrels and wound up with the nose of his plane in an ammunition dump, with the propeller cutting through boxes of .50-caliber cartridges. Nothing but good luck kept the dump from blowing up in his face. Four days later Faulkner taxied into the tail of a parked plane simply because he wasn't looking where he was going, and Colonel Wallace ordered him back from Midway for cracking up two airplanes — a thoroughly sufficient reason, after all. In addition, when the colonel reprimanded him, Cloudy got a bit too outspoken for a second lieutenant. So he was sent back for "further training, revocation of flight orders, and whatever action higher authorities deem necessary."

But instead of putting Faulkner through the fire when he reached Ewa, the authorities got his papers mixed up, and he was assigned not as a dive bomber but to a fighter unit. The first thing Cloudy knew, Bauer was sending him up in a Brewster on a familiarization hop to try a few stalls and spins.

"This Brewster wasn't bad for stunts, except that it didn't handle well in a dive, and it was a rotten fighter. However, that day it looked pretty hot to me. I'd flown an old Grumman F3F biplane in training and done those stalls and spins, but this Brewster was no dive bomber, and it scared me. I flew it up at a sharp angle till it stalled, then nosed over, gave her left rudder, pulled the stick back, and kicked her into a spin. She did everything too fast for me; my brains seemed to be lagging behind and wouldn't catch up. But when I pushed the stick forward and gave her opposite rudder, she came out of the spin, all right. After that, I had to do the same thing for an inverted spin, rolling her over on her back, and that left my brains farther behind than ever, and upside down, besides. I managed a fair landing finally and waited for the Coach to say something, because I knew that he'd counted every wobble I'd made in the sky. But he said nothing, and all at once I knew that he was on my side. He was, too, and made me navigation officer of the squadron, and then handed me Communications and Radio. Right after that the higher-ups discovered that I wasn't any fighter pilot at all, but just a dive-bomber pilot that needed discipline, so they reached out to grab me. But the Coach kept me in the clear and never would let me go."

Faulkner and Rogers are instances of the manner in which Bauer looked into the insides of a man. If he didn't like what he found, he knew how to draw and improve the hand. When he first called his lads together at Ewa, in one of the little huts which were assigned to the majors, "he called all his shots. He told us he knew that most of us were new at the game. He wouldn't expect us to beat the world in the beginning; he would teach us everything he knew. That would mean training, training, and more training. All he asked for was cooperation."

By the time the pilots of 212 finished their month at Tontouta, they had been hammered into shape as a unit. Something out of Bauer had been added to every man, and that extra, that plus, was what united them. They were "laying the same pattern of sky-trails" by the time they moved up to the completed airfield on Efate. Here the training was not so much under the eye of their commander. He was away for days at a time because his eye was needed on far-off islands to select sites for new fields and to give advice in many councils. Construction battalions were coming down into the South Pacific to increase the footholds from which the United States was at last to spring its counterattacks, and Bauer had to be strategist as well as tactician as he helped devise plans for the push northward toward Guadalcanal. Meanwhile, the training on Efate, under supervision of his executive officer Major Payne, who had been Bauer's wing man for a year and a half prior to the war, became more than a game. Constant air alarms were coming in, and the squadron was scrambled several times nearly every day to prepare itself for possible enemy action and make interception of all aircraft detected, friendly or otherwise.

A radar set had been established by Technical Sergeant Murrell on a mountain, hard for even a goat to climb, but Murrell had labored his nearly three hundred pounds up the difficult slopes and moved tons of equipment as well, so that on the height the radar would meet with no interference. Radar, long kept a profound secret, is now known to the world as the device that detects objects in the air by the reflection or "echo" from them of very short radio waves. This echo registers as a pulse on a screen calibrated to give range, elevation, and direction. If aircraft moved within 150 miles of Efate, the radar was sure to pick them up, and even the size of the force was indicated — a miracle of invention, a sort of tentacle that swept the skies and whose touch it was impossible to avoid.

This information, radioed down to Sergeant

DeBenedictis, the fighter director, led to the scrambling of the planes of 212. DeBenedictis had a plotting board on which he could note all the information sent down by radar, and it was he who kept in touch with the pilots after they were in the air, to make them aware of the movements of other planes. One important bit of information DeBenedictis and his radar could not provide, however, was identification of aircraft detected. That had to be done by pilots taking to the air and determining whether approaching planes were friend or foe.[1]

Of course, during this period there was increasing air traffic coming up from Australia and down across the Pacific from the States, yet radar on Efate never dared to take anything for granted for fear of another Pearl Harbor, on however small a scale. That was what kept 212 so constantly in the air, and it was one reason for the remarkable performance of the squadron when it joined battle. Aside from what radar and air-to-air identification of aircraft told them, and an occasional word from the Royal Australian Air Force base, 212 was living in the dark while the whole world was burning just over the horizon. As for the actual seeing of anything highly likely to involve the enemy, that was done through the eyes of Sergeant Woolley in his amphibian, as he ranged from Noumea to Guadalcanal and the Santa Cruz Islands, across many hundred miles of extra-salty sea that he had to fly by dead reckoning, without navigational aids and without a scrap of arma-

77

ment to put up a fight if an enemy scout made a pass at him.

On Efate at about this time Bauer was forced to ground a promising flyer, Staff Sergeant Mayhew, who found that planes were too slow for him. "He wanted a spaceship," Woolley said, "like Buck Rogers. Every time he came in, he left the palm trees waving behind him and gave a haircut to Corporal Wallace on the steamroller. The closer he was to the ground, the more he felt like doing gymnastics. The whole ground crew thought he was going to be one of the greatest aces that ever flew. But there was a bridge down there, and the boys used to lay bets about whether a plane could fly under it. Mayhew heard about the bets, and that was enough for him. So he dived his plane under the bridge. He bent the tail wheel on the riverbank and ground-looped on landing, dragging a wing tip. It pretty well killed the plane, but it didn't hurt Mayhew."

Planes were more valuable than pilots during the early days of the war, and Bauer couldn't risk losing any more of his, so Mayhew was grounded. Every morning thereafter Bauer made it a point to intercept Mayhew and lay on a full day's assignment of work, all kinds, good and bad. "At the end of this testing period, the Coach got us all together in the Ready Room one day, saying Mayhew had passed all the tests he had put to him, and it was up to us if he flew again, as we would be the ones he would be flying with." This was another example of the team spirit Bauer wanted his men to have. "We were unanimous in our approval, so Mayhew flew again — until he forgot to let his wheels down one day and did a beautiful belly-slide that didn't hurt the plane very much, but still you couldn't call it flying." That did it. Mayhew was grounded for good and did not get a chance to meet the enemy.

The pilots of VMF-212 were getting acquainted with the ground crew. They had had to service their own planes while at Tontouta — an excellent way to make oneself familiar with all parts of a ship, but a lot of greasy work, too — and they were glad to hand over these duties to experts. They also needed the entertainment that the ground crew lads provided. Corporal Cook was one of these with a pair of hands that knew how to box, and a pair of brains that knew how to grow wacky when he let them go. "We didn't have a bugle in the echelon but didn't need to blow reveille when Cook was there. He used to start hollering in the dark of the morning. About that time, the guards would come through beating a dishpan with a big spoon, but you couldn't hear the guards because Cook had started everybody hollering like roast turkey and a letter from home." Corporal Helm was another entertainer worth his weight in dollar bills as a morale builder. A big, husky fellow full of Texas, he had a strange knack of making a tune by rubbing the handle of a broom on the floor, and to that accompaniment he made up jingles and ballads on every name in the squadron. "Most of them you couldn't print, but they were sure good for a laugh and a holler down there in the jungle. When he and Sergeant Bledsoe weren't welding or making things to hold the job together, they were fighting one another. And when they weren't fighting, they were putting on a show for the whole gang."

The pilots found the ground crew a new and strangely interesting world, and by degrees they came to know the quieter figures, men with a silent devotion to their work, like Domeney, who with his crew strung telephone lines from radar on the mountain to all necessary points, sleeping out for days and coming in at last exhausted, plastered with caked and recaked jungle mud; or Rudolph "Spec" Elias, ready to slave at any work; or Guasticci, the electrician who could repair anything, including your watch; or Perry, who kept the wheels turning in Transportation, always covered with grease and a smile bigger than himself; or Technical Sergeant George Garner, who was always fixing the guns when they jammed in practice runs and keeping the ammunition at full supply; or Frederick Scroggins, with a heart far bigger than his body, full of devotion to the pilots and the whole squadron; or Doody, who was never wrong; or Hillbilly Dean, who sang the loudest song in camp.

It would have been hard to find 150 men who better represented the whole United States, particularly the tougher part of it, for these were volunteers, and the magnet of adventure attracts the true metal. Fifty percent of them were "characters," many with talents so young and so new that they had not yet arrived at any rating. Take the Los Angeles schoolboy James Milne, for instance. He was a lean, awkward youngster with the most innocent look in the world, but with a pair of hands that could do anything. Give him a coil of wire and a monkey wrench, and he'd repair a ship's engine. The boys called him Cheshire Cat because of his grin, which stayed on his face when he played poker with those who dared, because he was a real manipulator and only took on those who asked for trouble. He had keys and devices that would open any lock. No hour even in the wettest jungle could really be dull if it included Milne. He was only a private first class for the moment, but to the squadron he killed a more insidious enemy than the Japs, which was Time.

# Baptism of Fire

*eight*

★ The time had come for 212 to begin to send men into the action at Guadalcanal. The battle of the South Pacific was approaching its crisis, the moment when Americans would have to grapple with Japanese and fight it out at some distinct point, or else give up the war for the islands. Guadalcanal was the place. The Japs had their new airfield on that island almost functioning by July. It would be long enough for bombers soon, in spite of the pasting it got from our Army four-engine B-17 "Flying Fortresses" that flew up from the strip on Efate, now expanded to a fine fifty-eight-hundred-foot field. The Fortresses attacked the Guadalcanal field gallantly and did their best, but the trouble was that too many of their bombs dropped in nearby ocean or jungle. The pilots came back shaking their heads. Something was wrong. Something was very wrong with that high-altitude bombing.

"Then the Navy's carrier-based dive bombers went in, and that was a different story. By the time they got through dropping their stuff, the Guadalcanal airfield was packed with so many gaping craters that only an oversized kangaroo could have taken off across it." When the Jap planes were made homeless in this fashion, red-faced, amiable, but hard-as-nails Major General Alexander A. Vandegrift pushed in his Marines so suddenly that after landing on August 7, they had the all desired field in their hands by August 8. The neighboring island of Tulagi and two other objectives were being pocketed at the same time, not all so easily, but the clever Japs had been completely outfoxed at every turn, and so taken by surprise that they had to run for their lives, leaving half-eaten food on the tables of the officers.

Masses of invaluable equipment passed uninjured into American hands, also a large tonnage of food that included canned fruits and all manner of meats and fish. Without those Nipponese rations the hungry days to come would have been sheer starvation. And to wash the food down there was plenty of Japanese beer and champagne cider, for they had sent luxuries along with necessities to this farthest Pacific outpost from which they hoped to cut the throat of the long America-Australia line of communications. All their preparations had begun on a large scale, and permanence was clearly in their minds as they established themselves. As for the surprise attack, since Pearl Harbor they had done all the surprising. The shock to Jap morale was mortal. From that day to this they have vainly been trying to recover lost face. On Gavutu and Tanambogo, two nearby islets, they were holding out in caves, which the Marines blasted with dynamite and then hauled out the bodies like stunned fish from the sea. But Japan was not going to give up that priceless airfield on Guadalcanal without a fight; she began to send down the counterattack in waves.

The airfield was valuable in part because it was almost completed and must be kept out of American hands, in part because though little fighter strips may be laid down here and there, the level space for the big-bomber runways is rather a rarity in that part of the world. Guadalcanal, shaped like a crooked banana or "a sausage with a bellyache," is a ragged heap of green mountains and hills, but on the northern side of it, toward Tulagi, there is a smooth place between the Lunga and Tenaru rivers, and that was where the Japs had laid out their strip. It was a prize. It was one in a thousand out of the grab bag.

Jungle and coconut groves surrounded the field except for one sector where open meadow extended toward the background of hills, and the Jap could come overland, or by air, or by sea, hugger-mugger through the double darkness of night and the jungle, unless there were plenty of troops to stop him from all sides. The answer was brief: There were not enough troops. The Marine commandos, known as the Raiders,[1] had been killing out the Japs five to one, and even eight to one, but still more Japs were coming down. And they continued to carry their former glory, their former "face," with them, only slightly tarnished, so that a well-known American observer would remark, "There can be no question of our being better fighters than the Japs. The best we can possibly do is to be as good, and rely on our superiority in other departments of war to give us victory in the long run."

This observer knew what the Raiders had done to the Japs in the Solomons, cutting them down as wolves might kill foxes and coyotes, but still intelligent opinion was blinded by the triumphs of Jap treachery and tactics since Pearl Harbor; it was further persuaded by the indubitable fact that the Jap would fight till he died, and the other facts about the little fighters of Hirohito had not been added up. They didn't seem to make sense. The Raiders, using raw courage and keen intelligence, did things to the Japs which were not properly evaluated because the world was filled with the conviction that the Nips were the most deadly fighting machines in the world.

That was the situation when Captain John L. Smith, later Major and winner of the Congressional Medal of Honor, arrived on Efate with Marine Fighter Squadron 223. Eight of his pilots needed further training, so he took eight from Bauer under the leadership of Captain Everton and went on up to Guadalcanal; and thus nearly half of the first fighters to land on "the Canal" and hold a shield to the sky over the heads of the Raiders were from 212. That was August 20.

Momentous as that day was, it was a bit disappointing to the rest of 212, left behind on Efate. The entire squadron had been scheduled to be the first fighters to land on Guadalcanal. But since Higher Authority had decided otherwise, 212 had no choice but to obey.

Doc Everton had been flying for a dozen years, since he was a boy of seventeen and barnstormed around the country with an old ex-Marine flyer, keeping the plane clean and acting as general flunkey. That was how Everton learned to fly, and the passion never left his blood. That, and his ability to lead and command, was why Bauer sent him in advance with his seven pilots on the escort carrier Long Island, which also ferried Squadron 223 toward the Solomons.

Late of an afternoon they took off from the Long Island and flew toward Guadalcanal. "There were white clouds blooming in the wind," said Everton, "and plenty of sun, and I remember how darned peaceful the island looked, and beautiful and green, with meadow close to the beach. So I thought how lucky it was that if a fellow had engine trouble, he could land almost anywhere. But I later remembered that all we owned of that picture postcard was what you could cover with a postage stamp, and besides, what looked so smooth from high up could be soggy marsh or a firetrap of reeds if you settled down close to it."

As they came in they brought lighter hearts to those muddy and profane Raiders. "I just looked up and grinned till I felt the mud crack on my whiskers," one of them recalled, "it looked so damn good to see something American circling in the sky over the airfield. It was like being all alone, and then the lights come on, and you've got friends from home in the same room with you." And this was the beginning of a lasting comradeship based upon mutual respect. It was impossible to tell the pilots that the Raiders who were holding off the swarming Japs were not the bravest fellows in the world, and to the Raiders the chosen heroes were the pilots who kept swatting the Jap hornets out of the sky. Everton's leading division of four landed, taxied over to the edge of the palm grove, and changed the hard tail wheels which are best for landing on a carrier's deck for the softer ones needed on more yielding terrain. They had brought out sacks of food from the carrier, but when Everton turned to pick his up, it was gone. "Every man that's hungry enough is a thief," he grinned.

In the coconut grove, bedding was being distributed to the pilots, a Jap mosquito bar, two Jap blankets, plus directions to look for a vacant Nip tent. Everton found one with a battered top and no sides, but a roof is what makes a home. There were no cots, of course. Instead there were Jap bags made of woven rice straw, such as they used for sandbag emplacements, and these placed three long and two deep made up a bed. "There were no pillows, but on the whole it was damned thoughtful of the Japs."

That night the battle of the Tenaru started.[2]

Everton stayed in his tent with his .45 in one hand and a tin hat in the other, ready to start leaving with his shoes in one hand and the gun in the other if trouble came too close.

A man's first battle makes the kind of music that never can be forgotten, like a song that drives you crazy because it won't get out of the top of your head. Everton could hear the Raiders in the front lines open up with .50-caliber machine guns, holding them down for long bursts that made a deep-throated roar; the .30s had a sharper, more rapid and ringing patter. In between he made out the Jap 25-mm high-pitched reports, coming slowly. "They only fire at a certain slow rate. I don't know why. They must be built to save ammunition. Then our mortars began to toss shells across the river, and we heard them go whoomp, whoomp." Under the trees it was thick and black, but he saw the picture by the sounds.

There was quiet, after a time, but early in the morning the Japs tried to break through. "They would have gotten through before, everyone said, except that they didn't know the barbed wire was there until the barbs were tearing their flesh at the end of their first charge. So in the early morning they sneaked up again and tried to cut the wire, but they didn't know how to do this silently, and under their snipping the wires went ping, ping." Raiders, as everybody knows, can hit a sound as well as a sight, and they scythed those Nips down in solid swathes with machine-gun fire. In the dawn the river was loaded with the dead.

It seems to Everton that it was next morning, when he was sitting in his plane warming it up, that Captain Smith came running over with a map in his hands. He jumped up onto the plane and shoved the map under Everton's nose with his finger on the spot and said, "Just had a report that they are coming up the shoreline in landing boats and sending reinforcements to breach the line of the Tenaru. I want you to go out, investigate, and use your own judgment about strafing or returning."

There wasn't any need to explain the importance of the mission. The thin line of Marines around Henderson Field was always just a bubble, and once it was pricked the whole show was over, for the Japs were in floods, ready to stream through the smallest breach. Everton took off with three planes following him, Tex Hamilton flying his wing position, which means that he lay just to the right and a little behind. They swept across to the spot Smith had spotted on the map and found Jap landing boats scuttling along the shore and holding close to the overhanging trees. Some already were landing, but at a point where they had to come out into the open. Everton gave the word, and four planes dipped down to strafe.

The effect of the .50s is something that men accustomed to machine-gun fire in the first world war cannot understand. A slug that hits a man right will blow his body almost in two. Later, two

Jap destroyers were to be sunk with the help of concentrated fire from these weapons. What they did on this occasion to the landing boats was wonderful and terrible. After the first pass, the Japs were in the water trying to swim, with three of their boats sinking beneath them, and forty Japs to a boat. Some of them were dead from gunfire, some drowned, some made the beach. "But we left plenty of them wriggling around in the water in circles, minus an arm or a leg, I guess."

The second part of the play now opened. As the Japs struggled up the beach, soggy in the knees, weak as wet cats from what they had been through, the Raiders opened up from the trees beyond and drove them back toward the sea. More were coming in boats that managed to make the beach, the boats cluttered with the dead and sinking, with bullet holes bored up and down their length. And these new arrivals were picked up and herded forward together with the whole crowd of refugees by the blasting fire of the Grummans.

And as the herd started for the trees, the Raiders at leisure cut them down and rolled them in diminished lines back to the water. Some of them tried to use the heaped dead as sandbags, but they could not fortify themselves against fire from the air. One machine gun opened up desperately on the Grummans. "But Tex Hamilton dove at him, and that was that."

In the end, Everton said with dreadful and

military precision, "as there were no more targets available, I took my flight back to Henderson Field." On the beach the Japs were dead or swiftly preparing to die. No prisoners were taken on that bright morning, except those too badly wounded to destroy themselves. Smith reported later that a thousand had tried to land; eighty were saved for the doctors. As for the Raider loss, it was almost nothing, and the Grummans were not scathed — an ideal instance of the annihilating effect of ground forces and the air arm in cooperation. From the prisoners it was learned that they had been told that only a few Americans were on the island and that since they had white skins, they would surrender at once.

"But when they found out there was fighting, the Nips fought all right. But they have funny ways when they come to the pinch. I guess they can win in fine style, but when things go wrong they stop thinking. They go bulling ahead, showing their teeth, and their eyes crazy. You can't beat Raiders that way, but it's a shortcut to heaven and Hirohito, I suppose. They do everything in sequence, the way it was planned for them by their officers. If something fails in the sequence, they can't play the hand in a new way. They keep on playing bridge when the game has changed to poker. And that's just too bad."

One wonders how men in their first battle felt about the crimson beach and the twisted bodies that lay on it, but Everton said simply, "We'd heard a good deal about the Japs and their ways.

So nobody minded the picture."

VMF-212, however, began to make a name for itself on August 24 when a flood of Jap bombers and fighters came over Guadalcanal. Taylor, Massey, Freeman, McLeod, Bastian, King, and Hamilton were among those who took off toward the bombers from Henderson Field, and on this day McLeod, King, and Hamilton were blooded. The first two got a bomber apiece, and Hamilton shot down two Zeros. Four planes at first effort was a good start, but the day was a black one for 212. One of their best, Second Lieutenant Larry C. Taylor, had helped Rex Jeans of 223 shoot down a bomber, and then his luck ran out. "There's no use thinking forward. There's no use worrying. When your number is up, that's the end for you." So Taylor went down, but his unpaid account with Nippon would be settled over and over again before the game had ended on Guadalcanal.

It was at 4:20 on the afternoon of the twenty-fourth that the flyers were scrambled to meet this raid, in which the Japs lost seventeen planes, with Captain Marion Carl of 223, afterwards famous for his many victories, and Lieutenant Kenneth Pond, also of 223, credited with three apiece. A fact of overwhelming importance was that Jap bombers had not held grimly on to attack their target. They had been turned back by that slaughter in the air. Not a single bomb had fallen on the field.

The Japs were growing desperate now. The longer Henderson Field remained in the possession of the Americans, the more certainly the Americans would establish a growing and at last a superior air force on Guadalcanal. Ten minutes after midnight they sent in five destroyers to plaster the field. Three dive bombers flew out and bombed and strafed the Jap cans until they scattered away. The small guns of the destroyers were rather a nuisance than a serious threat to the field.

At eight on the morning of the twenty-fifth, news came that the first of the "Tokyo Expresses" was approaching. Four big transport vessels of from eight to fourteen thousand tons were coming down "the Chute" — the waterway from the north between the various islands, also called "the Slot" — at full speed, escorted very thoroughly by a light cruiser and from five to seven destroyers. "It seemed to us that this was it. I don't think there were two thousand Raiders on the island, and here was a whole damn Jap army coming down the Slot.[3] The way they pack troops on their transports, there's standing room only. All we had to stop that fleet was a handful of planes, and the boys were pretty glum. I remember a captain trying to cheer them up. He said a Raider is worth one and a half regular-line Marine infantrymen, and an infantryman is worth two Japs, so you can figure out how many fighting men we've really got here."

The Douglas SBD-3 Dauntless dive bombers of Squadron 232, also based on Henderson, put a deep dent into the approaching fleet despite the float-Zeros, equipped with pontoons, that protected the ships. "Lieutenant Fink hit the cruiser right on the bridge and blew the bridge and smokestack into the sea. The ship burned like a torch, and the flames and smoke were visible for miles away. Major Mangrum's bomb failed to release, but he returned and slid the bomb into a big transport and shook a crowd of Jap personnel into the sea." Then the dive bombers came safely home, harassed by the Zeros on the way.

At eleven of that busy morning, twenty-one Jap bombers came over the field, and the Grummans could not get at them because they were refueling. How many Jap transports had made it through to land troops on Guadalcanal nobody knew; but the boys were cheered that evening, in spite of the pasting the field had taken from the bombers, by word that torpedo-bombers from the carriers *Enterprise* and *Saratoga* had sunk the Jap carrier *Ryūjō*; of eighty Jap planes which attacked our ships, seventy-one had been shot down.

Squadron 212 had not made headlines on this day. On August 26, however, they added six more flags to their scoreboard, three going to Doc Everton. He took off on the wing of now Major Smith along with Lieutenant Corry and Tex Hamilton, and they contacted a flight of eighteen bombers. The other fighters, that day, had their hands full of Zeros; but under the attack led by Smith and Everton, the bombers turned away from Henderson Field, which meant that the main defense work was accomplished. The next part of the task was to whittle down the retreating Mitsubishis, who had dropped their bombs at random and were heading for the island of Malaita, northwest of Guadalcanal. The Americans came in on their flanks.

"The first plane I ever knocked down was at about twenty-four thousand," Everton said. "I had around two thousand feet of altitude on him, and I was from the side. It was a twin-engine Mitsubishi-97 with a crew of six or seven. All my hours in the air seemed to do me no good; all that practice in making smooth passes was thrown away. I had buck fever, and my whole ship was nervous under me. Instead of waiting for a good shot, I opened up at four hundred yards. You couldn't do anything at that distance except by luck, and my first tracers were behind the wing and fuselage. But as I closed in and the bomber grew bigger in the sights, I began to steady a little and smooth things out. I got up near and saw little pieces of metal flicking off."

The right engine of the Mitsubishi began to smoke; and when an engine begins to smoke, it's a fairly reasonable bet that the ship will not get home, not if there's a four- or five-hundred-mile run. Everton pulled up, ducked across the top of the Mitsubishi, did a wingover, and came in at him again. Everton felt quieter now. For the first time in his life he had put bullets into a living target; the shock of that was digested. And now smoothing out his pass in the true Bauer fashion, he slid steadily in on the bomber and did not fire a shot until he was inside three hundred yards.

He had chosen his angle of attack carefully, for these Mitsubishis had a fixed 25-mm machine gun in the tail, which cannot be turned from side to side but which can pour out a stream of bullets to the rear, the hope being that the enemy, trying for that mutually advantageous position, will plunge himself into trouble. In addition there is a turret on the top side, about in the middle of the fuselage, and this has an angle of fire of only a few degrees to either side. The plane therefore develops a blind spot on each side, and in this blind spot Everton pushed home his attack. Some pilots just throw a cone of fire at the enemy plane in general, but Everton is of the school that believes in using the sights of a gun. The three points of attack on a plane are, as a rule, the pilot's compartment, the engines, or the gas tank. As he shortened his range, Everton "saw a little flicker of flame alongside the fuselage by the gas tank, and all at once I felt pretty good. I pressed the attack right home, and the whole port side of the plane broke into smoke and flame. What made me feel good was not the thought of those Japs with smoke choking them and the fire jumping in their faces. Their number was up, and of course they knew it, but a pilot doesn't let himself think about that. He shoots at the plane, not the men in it. The plane is the thing that dies, not the crew. It's foolish to ask a flyer how many men he's killed; the count is only on the planes."

Everton knew he had his first score. In those two passes he had repaid his long and costly training over and over again. From this point forward in his life as a fighter pilot, everything would be decidedly plus. Now, as he saw the flames eat into the heart of the Mitsubishi, he pulled up and circled the bomber, watching it die in the air. After the first pass, it had begun to lose altitude and its position in the formation. Now, gradually, it fell off on the left wing and then dove straight at the ocean below. It was at twenty-three thousand when it burst into flame. Everton watched it down for three thousand feet, and then the bomber fell apart and turned into a shower of flaming junk. Five bodies appeared among those disintegrating elements, but not a single chute opened. "In those days they wouldn't bail out. A Zero pilot would, now and then, but most of them, too, preferred to die. Opening the parachute seemed to them like flying a white flag, I suppose, and they always had to save face. About the most honorable thing a Jap can do is die. And I hope that they keep right on feeling that way."

Everton turned the throttle wide open and began to overtake the bombers again. By this time his flight was whittled down to three Grummans, because Lieutenant Roy A. Corry, Jr., of 223, had not waited to get in the right position before he made his pass and had been sucked into the slipstream of the bombers — the slipstream full of bullets from those fixed machine guns in the tails of the Mitsubishis. Before he could duck out of that bad spot, his plane had been wounded fatally and spun down into the sea — a silver leap and flash of the water four miles below, like a signal — and there was another fine fellow gone.

Everton was up with the bombers now and had picked out his target on the right side of the formation. This time his pass was as steady as though he were at gunnery practice, the reason being that one victory in the air where you win or die can turn a flyer into a veteran. He was close in before he opened up, and one engine of the Mitsubishi began to smoke at once. It pointed its nose down and made a shallow turn to the right, apparently trying to make a forced landing on Guadalcanal. Everton whipped around to its starboard to force it back toward the sea, and the attack compelled the Mitsubishi to obey, like a great ox driven by a little sheepdog. Everton was trying for the pilot's compartment again, and the tracers were flying right into it. At twenty-two thousand feet the Jap made another left turn, put his nose down, and dove into the ocean.

By this time the bombers were heading for the northern tip of Malaita, hoping that the Grummans would run out of fuel. Passing Florida Island, Tex Hamilton was compelled by lack of ammunition to turn back with two of the bombers already shot down. Of the eighteen original bombers of that flight, some dozen remained, and still two little Grummans remained to worry them; opposite to Everton, Major Smith was tearing at them. Trying to give themselves more protection, the Mitsubishis fanned out into a line, flying abreast in groups of three, "which was just dumb tactics."

The cheerful voice of Smith came into the earphones of Everton, saying, "There's the table spread. Help yourself, Doc."

Smith started at one end of the bomber line; Everton attacked the opposite end. The Japs were filling the air with bullets, but they couldn't keep the Grummans from their blind spots. They were desperate now, and their leader thought up another foolish device. He had the formation begin flying up and down, tracing a wavy course through the sky, but that simply reduced their speed, ruined the aim of their gunners, and didn't bother the Americans at all. "But that's the way with them. If they're cornered, they're apt to think of the worst maneuvers first."

Smith and Everton were in on their flanks again. Everton's bomber began to smoke. He pulled up for another pass as it fell behind and began its down-run along the hill of the sky. Everton thought it might be trying to make a landing on Malaita and started a slicing dive from the starboard side, cutting across its path, but then he saw Smith closing in on the same target and so left the plane in his hands.

Everton continued after the other bombers, and presently he cut another ox out of the herd, wounding it to the heart with pass after pass until the bomber dove straight in, leaving a long exclamation point of smoke standing in the air.

By this time the bomber flight was turning left beyond the northern tip of Malaita, presumably to make for their base, which may have been much farther north at Rabaul. By that tactic they enabled Everton to make a shortcut, and presently he was above them at twenty-eight thousand. They were in sight of Santa Isabel Island when Everton made the Bauer overhead pass on one of them. Once more the big victim began to throw out the familiar streak of smoke as Everton came smoothly into the target. It lost position in the formation, but in making a second pass Everton found all his guns jammed but one. He was eighty miles from home, with only twenty gallons of gas left, and his latest target had already begun the long downward slant toward the sea, smoking furiously. It would not count as a score unless it were seen to strike the ocean, but Everton wisely turned back to Henderson Field.

"Probables never are added into your score. A plane has to explode in the air or hit the sea or smash into the ground. But if it's smoking from both engines and has five hundred miles to fly before it's home as it disappears in the clouds, it's simply nothing but your hard luck. That's the rule of the game, but it is mighty hard on some of the boys. Look at Bastian, a beautiful smooth flyer and a fine shot. He was only three times in contact with the enemy; he shot one Zero down, and he set two others smoking, but his score is just one. Everybody in the squadron knows that he really got three, but the official score is one."

Everton got back to the field to hear a fine horror story from Major Smith. The major had run out of ammunition in making his last attack, so he flew into the blind spot of the bomber and kept along beside it, to look things over — a very cool procedure on the major's part. As he drew in he saw that the gunner in the top turret was apparently dead. He could not see the pilot in the forward compartment. No one sat at the controls as the ship voyaged along, smoking badly, gradually sinking on the long incline toward the sea. It came over the major that everyone in the Mitsubishi was dead except the little gunner in the tail compartment, and he was frantic as a rat in a trap, clawing around and trying to get out. But he couldn't do it, and at about three thousand feet above the sea the whole glass cage he was in broke off and plummeted into the ocean. The plane went on in its long, soft glide and sliced into the sea farther off.

"We had knocked so many Japs out of the sky, time after time, that they would send nothing over for two or three days at a stretch, and then they'd come back with a fresh layout. Our opinion was that when the Japs got home, they never were all pooled at one field but split up into sections, so that the ground force never could tell just what the losses had been, and of course the pilots were trained not to talk. What the Japs know is the hooey they hear over their radios. For instance, during these days on Guadalcanal we'd pick up

Jap broadcasts that told about American battle-ships and cruisers, heavy and light, and whole flocks of destroyers, and scores of planes that were being sunk or knocked out of the sky day after day. Those people know how to add, and after a while they must realize that they've been fattened on lies for years. But the Jap pilots could talk a little to one another. A captured flyer told some of our intelligence officers that they called Guadalcanal Death Island, or the Island of No Return."[4]

# More of 212 Joins the Battle

*nine*

★ By September 1, Everton and the others from 212 who had fought under Major Smith had been relieved. Up from Efate came the original eight members of 223 who had remained for further training under Bauer, and it was a couple of weeks later before more pilots from 212 got into action. Payne led this new group. They came up on the carrier *Wasp*: Drury, Conger, Haring, and Chamberlain. It was a beautiful ship. The food was glorious. There was plenty of soap and hot water, and the Marines were glad they were a branch of the Navy. But the crew of the *Wasp* was not so happy. One sailor said, "We don't know what we're doing out here. We're just cruising back and forth and back and forth, waiting for a couple of tin fish to be thrown into us. We cruise twenty-four hours one way, and then we turn around and cruise twenty-four hours the other way, and the Japs are sure to find us sooner or later." They were found, in fact, soon after.

The knowledge that they were under full steam toward action made this the first big moment in the life of Conger, who was to be the leading ace of 212, next to Bauer himself. Conger is a five-foot-seven wedge of whalebone and India rubber, made to give and receive shocks. He has an eagle's straight-drawn brow, and the bright eye of an eagle also, and he has dreamed of flying since he was old enough to make plane models. He remembers how Major Payne and the carrier pilots lectured them the night before leaving the *Wasp* on how to take off from the ship, something in which they lacked practice. He remembered hotcakes for breakfast the morning of September 13, real hotcakes made with eggs, not those leathery fabrications of Scheinost back in Efate.[1] Their course had been determined the night before, Major Payne plotting it as the others followed, each putting it down on his chart board.

In the morning they were up long before dawn to check their planes. The oil had to warm up to 60 degrees and have a pressure of 90 pounds; the fuel pressure must be 15 pounds. There was a special routine for checking the oxygen, which must register 1,500 pounds on the gauge; the generator needed a look and also the propeller. They used Curtiss electric props that sometimes went haywire and did not make the proper number of revolutions per minute. "On automatic, the prop changes its pitch according to the speed of the plane and the density of the air, but this needs the work of a motor, and to save the motor the best idea is to operate the prop pitch manually by variometer most of the time." There is a long list to read off before the check is complete, and a man who trusts his memory in the morning may be a dead man before night.

"I start my own engine because my life depends on it," said Conger. "I check my chute, my life jacket hanging on the gunsight, see if my safety belt fits. I would always sit on my chute and fasten the safety belt tight over my lap. Would I do these things every day? You're damn right I would. Most of the pilots are careful, but when you're fighting you can't be too careful. I take more pains now than I did a year ago. Maybe if I get older I'll be careful all the time. On this particular morning it was hard to take the time for that checkover because I was eager, just eager to get in there; and it was tense, like waiting for the first whistle of a football game. By seven o'clock it was getting warm, with the sun well up. I revved my engine up to takeoff rpm and manifold pressure, holding my brakes, and when I got the signal from Fly One I released my brakes and started rolling down the flight deck. It's all as close to me as yesterday, the feel of the air and the sun, and thinking about Guadalcanal that lay off there, somewhere. About two-thirds of the way down the deck, I popped my flaps, because that gives you more wing surface and lift. And so she took off in good style."

The next day the boys of 212 learned that the *Wasp* had been sunk by Jap submarines shortly after their takeoff. So near and yet so far away.[2]

They rendezvoused and flew ahead up the channel between Florida Island and Guadalcanal, the islands looking mountainous and green. Two hours later they were circling for recognition over Henderson Field, named for a Marine pilot killed in the Battle of Midway,[3] and then landing with Major Payne in the lead. They had come down on the bomber strip of the field, only to learn that the fighter strip immediately adjacent had been commissioned that very day. So they hopped over to it. An alert came in almost at once. Forty-five minutes after reaching Guadalcanal, they were in the air to fend off enemy planes. At twenty thousand feet Payne's guns were all right. At twenty-five thousand they were frozen; at any rate, not one of them would work. He had to bring back to the strip what was left of his flight. But Second Lieutenant Richard D. Haring had gone in, apparently from oxygen trouble, and not a single Jap had had to pay for this loss.

While his guns were being fixed by Ordnance, Payne looked up Colonel Bill Wallace, commanding Marine Aircraft Group 23, which included dive bombers as well as Fighter Squadrons 223 and 224, and reported that he had no orders except to bring in the pilots from the carrier, but that he would like to stay and pick up some battle experience. Wallace told him to join up with Major Smith of Squadron 223. Payne had lived with Smith back at Ewa; now he found him loaded down with buckets of glory but still wearing the same size hat.

Just then the planes were scrambled again.

Conger said, "I was standing around in front

of the Ready Tent. I'd been up on the first hop but couldn't make a contact. Now I heard the telephone ring in the tent and somebody answer it, and then they were calling, 'Scramble everything! Tokyo Express!'

"Everybody ran out, and some of them jumped into jeeps to get to their planes. I was terribly excited. I hoped it would be my real chance to draw blood, and that was what I wanted: the blood. You get tired imagining that a sleeve is really an enemy plane. You get tired of making passes on friendly craft, and you get hungry for the real thing; you get hungry for it."

He joined up on two other pilots after the take-off, and they went to twenty-five thousand feet. Conger could hear over his radio, "Bombers approaching from 270 degrees, forty miles. . . . Bombers still coming from 270 degrees, thirty miles." And then: "Flight of Zeros coming five minutes behind bombers, course 270 degrees."

Finally, the whole horizon filled with planes. There were fifty-six of them, twenty-six bombers and thirty Zeros to give plenty of protection. There were so many, and so near, that Conger couldn't believe for a moment that these were really Jap planes. Conger's trio couldn't get in position for overhead passes, so they peeled off in high-side runs. As Conger started he looked across the formation and saw four other Grummans just completing their runs and three bombers falling in smoke.

"They were Mitsubishi-97s, like our B-26s but

bigger. I'd seen the Zeros before I got into action — brown, with a big red ball painted on each wing — but I didn't notice them now as I started my pass. There were enough bombers to fill my eye. I was too excited, and I guess that magnified the bombers, but I must have opened at 450 yards, which is a lot too far off. But as I closed in I saw my tracers going apparently right in front of the wings, which means they were going right into the wings; when they seem to be hitting the wing, they're actually going behind it.

"The left engine began to smoke, not gradually but with a big black puff. I fired a long burst, and the left engine began to flame; then the whole plane was on fire — bing, just like that. It just fascinated me. The bomber had looked so big I didn't see how I could do anything to it with a little Grumman. I was watching the Mitsubishi fall when all of a sudden my whole windshield disintegrated right in front of me. I felt a sharp pain in the right side of my head, and my left foot went kind of numb. Glass blew all over the cockpit. Something got in my eye.

"I knew somebody had me right, so I did a half-roll and got out of there, straight down for a couple of miles. There was nothing behind me when I leveled off and looked things over. There was glass all around me. The bulletproof windshield was a mass of cracks. My left eye was pretty bad, and there was a slug of metal sticking into my left shoe. The prop felt funny, too. There were three bullet holes in it, I found later. But that's one of the things to remember: how that bomber had just started to go to hell, and then blam! and my whole damn plane was caving in on me. It left me a little woozy.

"I landed and taxied over to the side of the field, and a couple of mechanics came out and asked if I'd made contact with the bombers. I said I had, and they'd made contact with me, too. The mechanics walked around to the left side of the Grumman and said, 'Jeez, they certainly have!' They'd peppered me. Back toward the tail of my plane there were a bunch of six-inch holes. The radio equipment in the fuselage was all blown to hell, and evidently a Zero had made a high-side pass on me. Major Payne came over then and took me up to report."

He had bad news to tell Conger on the way. Lieutenant Clair C. Chamberlain was gone. He had been sent to make contact with the bombers. Then Zeros jumped him, and last seen, his plane had been in a long dive that probably ended with him going straight in. It seemed the blackest of all days for the squadron.

That evening, just after supper, a dive bomber came in with a smashed radio. At any rate, it paid no attention to radio warnings from the field, where the operator was screaming his head off to warn the bomber that two float-Zeros were sailing through the sky above him. The American pilot went on serenely, dropping his flaps to make a leisurely landing. And then one of the Zeros peeled off, settled on the dive bomber's tail, and shot him down with one burst. The bomb he was carrying exploded as he struck the ground and blew the plane into a cloud of black smoke with a red smear somewhere in it.

"The Zeros got away. If they had anything like an even start, they always could get away from any of the planes we had in those days. It made everybody pretty mad, but there was nothing to be done. After this incident the dive bomber's rear-seat gunner always faced to the rear with his guns at the ready until safely on the field.

"The next morning there was another kind of a show, though. I watched some big transport planes, DC-3s (civilian name for the R4D–3), load up with wounded and take off to carry them back to Efate. It took extra armor-plated nerve to be the pilot of a DC-3 in a combat zone. Those planes will carry a lot of tonnage, but they're slow, they make a big target, and there's not even a popgun for defense. Well, when this flight of big whales got into the air, up came half a dozen of those float-Zeros I was telling you about. They must have been sitting on the water off the coast waiting for something just like this, and when I saw them streaking across the sky for those transports it made me sick at my stomach, because I knew what was going to happen. I *almost* knew, but not quite. Up there in the clouds was a dawn patrol the Japs hadn't counted on. It was made up of pilots from Fighting Five, a Navy squadron, and they dropped down on those damned Zeros and got every one of them before a single bullet could hit one of our transports full of wounded. It was the finest thing you ever saw. You know, there's something about the Navy. The Army is all right. The Army is fine. The Army is wonderful. But a Navy flyer is something else again. Somehow they get in there, and they're punching all the way."

Jap pressure was increasing on Guadalcanal, now. Conger and Drury moved their beds out of the coconut grove and moved into a slit trench with "I" Battery of the Eleventh Marines. They were received like brothers, for the American Marine, that strange creature to whom a fight with anyone is chewing gum and candy, is nevertheless able to know and cherish his own.

"We'd been used to quiet nights down on Efate except for the four-motored mosquitoes zooming and diving on us. Up here at Henderson Field it was quite a contrast. The nights were full of tracer bullets from the Jap ground forces, streaks of light going every which way like streamlined fireflies, but the Raiders kept things in hand by night, and our planes could shoo the bombers away by day, so it was turn and turn about, though the Raiders did the biggest turn, for my money. At first I had a little trouble sleeping in the middle of that show, but after a while it was all right. I just figured that when my number is up I'm going to get it, sleeping, flying, or whenever. When you get things worked out like that, you can relax a little."

# A Couple of Close Calls

## ten

★ There was a dull period that nobody could account for, unless the Japs were running out of planes or trying to dig up a batch of pilots who didn't know what happened to planes that tried to bomb Henderson Field. Whatever went on for the Raiders, there was little to do in the air except to talk about the way Major Smith had run up his score to nineteen or twenty on his way to that Congressional Medal.

There had been one dash of strikingly good news for 212. It received a man back from the dead; Chamberlain returned.

In that fight on the thirteenth he had been making a pass at a bomber when a Zero got on his tail and began to fill his plane full of holes. He dived out of trouble and pulled level at three or four thousand feet. There his engine cut out. A bullet may have sliced through an oil line. Anyway, he made a landing out there in the sea. When he pulled his rubber boat out, he found it was shot into a sieve, so he popped (inflated) his life jacket. For fifteen hours, blown back by the wind and the waves, he was in the water swimming for an island that seemed to get far-

112

ther and farther away. "And that takes guts. That's when the weak sisters give up. They fold, and they die. But this Chamberlain was one of the real ones, so he kept slogging along even when he'd stopped hoping." The point of importance was that he *did* reach the island. He had a small bottle of brandy along, and that warmed him up and gave him strength for the final pull. Then he was on the island for five days with coconuts for food. A dive bomber rendezvousing over the spot happened to see him, by the sheerest chance in the world, so they sent out a Duck and picked him up and brought him back, fifteen or twenty pounds lighter than he had been. He fought hard to be kept on Guadalcanal and be given another whack at the Japs, but his condition was too bad, and he was evacuated to Efate in one of the big DC-3s.

On September 27 the bombers were back, two flights of nine each with thirteen Zeros escorting, and the air over Guadalcanal bloomed with action once more. Major Payne went up with Conger, Drury, and Kenneth D. Frazier of 223. "One hell of a man, that Frazier, believe you me." Conger can remember every cloud in the sky, as they climbed up into it, for as he says, you don't forget your fighting days, particularly the ones in which you shot down an enemy. Furthermore, by this time the world had its eyes firmly fixed on Guadalcanal and the stand the Marines were making there; and some consciousness had come to the fighters themselves that they were making history, like athletes in a huge stadium with a hundred thousand pairs of eyes fixed upon them, except that here the stadium was the sea, the jungle, the blue sky of the Solomons, and the audience was counted invisibly, not by thousands but by tens of millions; and a stern joy was growing up in American hearts at home. And to the Axis Powers there was coming the cold realization that their propagandists had lied about Uncle Sam. He was not a soft old man but, once roused, a wicked and wily fighter, as always.

When Conger's flight got up to the altitude of the bombers, and off to one side of them, the escorting Zeros started dropping on the Grummans — and that was the classical pattern of the Guadalcanal air fighting: Jap bombers, Grummans edging above them for a pass, and Zeros as masters of the upper sky sliding down whenever and wherever they chose. The Americans had nothing in the air that could stay with them when it came to straightaway flying.

Conger got separated from the rest of his flight. "That's very bad. You never should get split up. I was watching the Zeros coming down and not paying enough attention to where the rest of the boys were going. I was too inexperienced. I was too green to remember everything that the Coach had been hammering into our heads. Pretty soon I found myself scissoring with a Zero. That is to say, he had the altitude to keep diving at me, and I kept turning into him, trying to stay behind and below. We scissored five or six times, and every time I made a sharp, steep bank I lost altitude. Altitude is what pays off in an air fight, and this looked bad. He forced me to keep making those quick turns to keep him off my tail, and with each turn my plane shivered and shook and lost altitude. It was hell.

"He passed above me and did a steep wingover. I dived and started to climb. It wasn't an intelligent thing to do, but I was lucky. He couldn't quite get his guns on me. Then he did the damnedest thing you ever saw. He came down from above and behind, and instead of riding it out on my tail and filling me full of bullets, he let himself go too fast so that he went by me. He should have dodged off to one side and got out of there, but instead of that the fool rose right up under my nose and did a roll.

"What was he trying to do? Impress me with his gymnastics? I don't know. Apparently those fellows had been told that they were the best flyers in the world, and so they were like little children with toys; they had to show their tricks when they had an audience. Or maybe he thought I couldn't hit him if he kept his plane tumbling like that. As a matter of fact, he was just making himself a bigger target. I used a three-second burst, and he was dead before I stopped firing. We had scissored all the way down to eight thousand — to show you how he had been driving me into the ground — but even eight thousand is a long way when you're looking down. He made a splash no bigger than a porpoise. Then he was just part of the soup.

"During the scissors I'd seen some Zeros over Florida Island circling above me. Right after this fellow went down, I heard and saw bullets going into my right wing. It looked as though every time I got my attention fixed on a target, some Jap got his attention fixed on me. I dodged into a cloud and went on instruments in the fuzz and the dark. When I came out, I was right on the tail of a Zero. He couldn't have been fifty yards away. Not that far, even. He was sitting in my lap. I just boresighted him, squeezed the trigger, and waited for him to fly into bits. But not a single gun would fire! Their fire had smashed one of my guns, or maybe the electrical system went wrong. But that was my last chance that day."

In the air at the same time was Second Lieutenant Frank Drury of 212, tall, handsome, his face marked by the double scar of the wounds he had received the month before, a lad with a dull, dreaming eye that kindled at moments with dangerous light. He came from a Missouri farm and a Baptist background. "Most of the fellows got rather religious, particularly under shellfire, which was pretty trying. We saw a few who went a bit off the rocker about religion, but none of the 212 pilots got too excited, I'd say. Still, there was a lot of praying, and I've seen men thumbing through a Bible in a foxhole where it was too dark to read a word." Drury grew up with the modest ambition of being a teacher in a country school, but when he got further along in his studies he discovered aviation, and the fire began to consume him. He had struggled through the usual training period, making little or no apparent progress, and then all at once he got the hang of it. "One day I wasn't any good and the plane was a machine; the next day it knew what I was thinking about. That made me cocky, and it took some experience before I realized that I had to keep on learning to the end." To many, Drury was the most brilliant, the most reckless of the whole outfit; to the ground crew particularly he and Tex Hamilton were the flying aces, perhaps. But what seemed reckless taking of risks to the ground crew was in reality the sharp flying of a man absolutely sure of his ship.

Life was all plus and no minus for Drury when he came to Guadalcanal, for he should have been dead in August. He had been at Espiritu Santo on a standby alert at the bomber strip whose site Bauer had selected. That was where he first saw natives wearing nothing but belts of woven grass, real sunsuits. "There were real cannibal tribes back in the hills, and even the people along the shore seemed to know about the idea. White men, they said, tasted like horse meat. They weren't a bad lot but were very simple, loved to sing, and never stopped wondering at the planes. They called the Flying Fortresses 'Big Pigeons.' " At Espiritu, trouble came to Drury in a strange way.

They were sitting around one day when they heard a great explosion out to sea, and Major

117

Payne flew out in a fighter to see what the trouble might be. He found that a destroyer had been leading a ship loaded with aviation gas toward the island, unaware of a newly laid minefield. One of those mines had split the destroyer *Tucker* right in two, and two ends of her were sticking out of the water when Payne flew over. He saw another destroyer, the *Breeze,* ten miles out, and it looked like a sure thing that the following transport and its cargo of gasoline would be blown to bits in the minefield unless it got a warning. Payne returned and picked Drury to take messages out to the ships, and they fixed up two watertight cans he was to drop. The *Breeze* on patrol out at sea had helped to lay the minefield; she could show the transport through. And then Payne flew back in the Duck to pick up survivors of the *Tucker* and tow their life rafts to shore while Drury went out and passed the *Breeze* at no more than a hundred knots, to make sure of dropping the cans right. He tossed a can overboard as close as he could, but he had been paying too much attention to this job and not enough to the decreasing momentum of the plane with its flaps down. As he opened the throttle again, his left wing dropped.

"I tried to pull it up, gave right rudder, and poured the coal into it, but it didn't right enough. I hit the water still turning. The left wing ripped off like paper, and the plane dove right in. When I hit, it was like a board had slammed me in the face. There wasn't much consciousness left in me

118

to tell what happened. The gunsight wasn't padded with rubber, and it slashed my cheek; my goggles made the cut over my eye. I banged my right shoulder on the open hatch, too. Then I was thrown clear of the plane, ending up in the water.

"It just happened that the officer in command of that ship was a rare bird. As I came down the starboard side of the destroyer, he saw that I was going to crash. The time it took him to run across the bridge, the plane and I were out of sight, and there was only an oil slick left on the surface of the water. That would have been enough for most men. They would have crossed me out as one more casualty, but this fellow was real Navy. He got a boat into the water in no time at all and jumped in to take charge of it himself."

By that time Drury had floated up to the surface, but everything was a fog. "The destroyer was over there, but it didn't mean much to me. I knew I was in the water, I knew I had crashed, but nothing was important except to try and keep my head above water. It seemed better to rest and stop struggling, but something kept me moving. My parachute was dry, and as I hadn't unbuckled it, it pulled my rear end up and dunked my head into the sea. I was weighted down with my helmet, goggles, my gun, and my heavy shoes. I hadn't the wits to get rid of these things, and though I had a life jacket on, I didn't think of inflating it. I finally realized that I had to unbuckle my parachute so I could inflate my Mae West, but then I passed out."

They saved Drury, but it was a very close thing. The skipper of the destroyer dived from the boat and got our flyer. The last Drury could remember was the salt water coming through his nostrils and his vague effort to swallow it in order to keep it out of his lungs. So they hung him over the rail of the boat and let him drain like a wet cloth on the way back to the destroyer. Then they brought him around and sewed him up.

# The Coach Scores Again and Again

*eleven*

★ The wounds of Drury were healed by the time he flew into Guadalcanal and went up into the air to intercept the Japs that day at the close of September. The Zeros dropped on him as on Conger, and he dived away to evade them. He tried to join up on another Grumman as he came out of his dive, but he was going so fast that the other Grumman joined up on him instead. Two planes in the air were five times as safe as one.

They started climbing upstairs. Drury saw the bombers go to the southwest corner of the island, so he believed that if the two of them could climb fast enough, they could head off the Mitsubishis on their way home. It was a humid day, and each plane was leaving in the air a trail of congealed moisture (contrail), so that Drury could see where all the dogfights were going on, writing their own descriptions at large in the sky. Sixty miles from Guadalcanal the two of them got ahead of the bombers and above them, so that it was possible for them to peel off in overheads. Drury got in position with a perfect boresight and slid down in a smooth pass without, it seems, the nervous

121

fluster that preceded the blooding of other members of the squadron. Perhaps his crack-up in the sea had served as the first battle to draw off that uneasy effervescence of the spirit. There was one very odd feature of this fight: the bomber broke into smoke and flames not at the roots of the wings, where the gas tanks were, but in the tail. It was going down like a rocket, spitting fire out of its rear end, and so straight on into the sea.

September 27, however, was a mere warming up, a favorable augury for the twenty-eighth, which was a bigger day in the history of Guadalcanal. For one thing, Bauer appeared. Major Payne said, "That day was Sunday, and Joe came out to the fighter strip and looked at the sky like a wild duck with a clipped wing. His business was on the ground, not in the air, but he had been holding himself in for a long time. He asked Major Robert E. Galer, commander of 224, if there was a spare plane around, and Galer gave him one. 'They'll come over today just because you're here,' Galer said to him. 'I know your luck. It's your first chance to make a score, and you never waste time.' Well, it was just that way. In a minute or so, radar was telling us about a fine sky full of Japs that were coming in, and then there was Joe Bauer hitched into Galer's outfit and climbing into the sky. Twenty-five bombers and thirty Zeros were zooming in and were intercepted before they had a chance to damage the field. Of course, Joe got a score for himself, and it was one of the outsize Mitsubishis at that. He just got up there to Guadalcanal, popped into a plane, shot down a Jap, landed, and grabbed a transport plane back to Efate. It was a real Bauer stunt, a sort of game, a sort of joke, and I'll bet he was grinning all the way back to the New Hebrides. If he'd ever had a steady run of chances against the Japs, who can guess how many of them he would have had on his score? As it was, he was only four times in the air, and he grabbed eleven. Nobody ever topped that."

It was Payne's chance for first blood also that day. He went up with the outfit of Marion Carl of 223. Major Smith's gang was ahead, but Carl cut inside them and put his flight in perfect position for runs on the bombers. Payne picked out a bomber toward the tail of the formation, opened up too early, as nearly everyone did on the first pass, then checked himself and closed to effective range. He was settling down on this bomber and giving it punishment when another bomber came in under him from the rear, so close they nearly collided. The move was so quick and the change so sudden that Payne hardly had time to squeeze the trigger and get in one burst on the second plane. The sky is like that in war: now empty as a desert, now full of whale-shaped bombers, now alive with fighters as quick and savage as thin-sided barracuda.

Payne dived on past the formation and pulled up for another go at it — which is the usual procedure, for of course a dive generates extra speed to help the plane coast up the next hill of the sky. He was around sixteen thousand now, and there were no Grummans near him, whereas there had been an eager crowd of fighters before. He had kept his eyes too closely fixed on his job, and the result was that he knew not even the direction in which his friends had disappeared. "A good fighter pilot has extra eyes on top of his head, and under his chin, and behind his head, too. Besides, he keeps moving like St. Vitus dance, because he's living in four dimensions, and his death may come at him from any of the lot."

The Grummans were gone, but they had left the bomber formation thoroughly broken up. The Mitsubishis were diving for clouds, completely demoralized. Payne came in on one of them with a full-deflection beam shot and got sucked in slightly behind, almost into, that slipstream of bullets which the Mitsubishis pour out behind them. But Payne suddenly realized that the tail gunner was not sending out this monotonous flood. Perhaps he was dead. The major closed right in from behind, but the bomber hit a cloud, and the Grumman went in after him. He circled all sides of that cloud, then, but the Mitsubishi had dissolved itself in the sky spaces as any plane is apt to do. In twenty seconds a ship may have slipped two miles away, and behind all sorts of formations of clouds or dimming mist. Payne was down over Savo Island now, so he shoved off for Henderson Field, feeling pretty sour. He was damning the other two planes that had gone into the action first with him. They weren't 212, but the idea always should be to stick together. Then the man ahead may deflect or turn or slow up an enemy, and the fellow behind is perfectly set to shoot him down.

Payne claimed the first bomber he made the pass on, because he'd seen the ship start falling apart. Afterwards the man who flew wing on him said that the second bomber he got the burst into had also practically exploded in the air. But by that time Payne had been too far away on his course, and unless claims are filed immediately, they're no good. So that day he could put only one flag on the scoreboard.

Drury got his number two on this day, at the same time, but it is curious to note how the picture differed from his angle. He had joined up on Major Smith and followed him into position so that every man of the flight got a perfect high-side dive. By the time Drury went down on them, the whole formation of bombers had been shot away up to the middle of it. Except for the after portion, the rest were streaking down through the air in smoke and flames, and the remnants were refugees that had jettisoned their bombs and were turning in a desperate drive for home. Drury poured in his fire so that the tracers were converging just in front of the nose of his chosen bomber, and the plane lifted its head like a poling [spyhopping] whale, as though it wanted to look around at the trouble it had found; then it went down to crash.

Of twenty-five sleek bombers aimed at Henderson Field on this day, twenty-three were knocked out of the clouds, known casualties, and it is doubtful if any of the lot managed to return to their base. "It was a rotten day for Tojo. It evened things a little for what he did at Pearl Harbor."

What made it more satisfying was that every American pilot returned safely from this holocaust.

On October 2 Bauer was back from Efate with more of his pilots and thirsty for action — which was really taboo, his ground responsibilities being so heavy. However, it was manifestly impossible for him to keep out of the air now and then.

The very next day he formed up with Marion Carl, and their section of six planes dived on ten Zeros. "Three went down at the first stroke, and Carl with the other Grummans shoved off, which left Bauer alone to play with the seven remaining Zeros. Only three escaped. It was simply a question of flawless gunnery and perfectly smooth passes." He went in like a skater on flawless ice, drawing a straight line until he had his enemy in perfect focus for his guns. Then a burst or two ended the business, and as the Zero fell off on a wing or simply disintegrated before this unendurable concentration of firepower, Bauer was already after the next victim. "Ever see a bull terrier kill rats? They give them one grip and a shake that breaks the neck, and then grab the next one like lightning."

This burst of brilliant action was not what dwelt

126

in the mind of Colonel Bauer that night. Before the end of the fighting, he had seen an American parachute dropping over the water. "Suddenly a Zero came out of nowhere and opened up with a very long burst on the parachute. This infuriated me. I went after that Zero with gusto."

There is a good deal behind that description. In his earlier attacks on the four Zeros, all his guns except one had jammed after he had knocked down his third plane. With that single gun he had downed the fourth Jap fighter, but a flyer with only one gun active is like a man with one arm tied behind him and the other in a splint. However, the rage of Bauer was uncontrollable when he saw the Jap machine-gunning a helpless American in the air. He forgot the odds and went at that Zero in a screaming dive. It was Frazier, one of the best of Smith's fine flyers, who was dangling from the parachute.

Pop Flaherty of 212, who had been in the air that day for the first of his combat flights, said, "Bauer got on the tail of that Zero and started him smoking right off. A Zero can fly rings around any Grumman Wildcat that ever was, but the Coach had injured this fellow so badly that he was able to stay up there on his tail while the Jap lost altitude. The Coach kept slamming into him with his one gun until he remembered the man in the parachute and went back to see that he was taken care of when he landed in the sea. That Zero never got home. But there was a destroyer cruising around, and it picked up Frazier from the water when Bauer marked the spot by zooming around in the air.

"The Coach was the last to land, and we were waiting for him. We knew what he could do in the air, but this was the first time he'd had a chance to show his stuff to the world. When he came in, his engine was flaming out from time to time — burning gasoline was what it was. He taxied it back to the line. He cut the switch. It was still burning like a son of a gun. They had to put out the blaze with fire extinguishers. The Coach came roaring in like a happy boy, shouting that he had gotten five of the sons of bitches. He was plenty excited. He hardly knew what he was doing, and he'd left his parachute on instead of leaving it in the plane.

"We were terribly happy because of what he'd done, but we couldn't help laughing a little to see him so excited. He didn't think he was. In fact, he explained to us that he was as calm as he'd ever been in his life."

He was still explaining this when a mechanic came up to him with a grin and said that he'd landed with his high-altitude supercharger on as well as the auxiliary fuel pump. Both should be cut off under fifteen thousand feet.

"The Coach didn't excuse himself. He just laughed about it. I never saw a man who loved a fight the way he did. He was drunk with it. It was shining out of him. After a fight he was always a little crazy with the excitement, and it burned us up to see the effect on him. It made you want to get up there and breathe the same extra-special ozone that he always seemed to find when he was in action."

This was October 3. A month and twelve days later, Bauer was to be posted missing in action. Already he had done a great deal, and yet the greater part of his fighting life was to be compressed into the few weeks that remained.

# An Encounter with the Japanese Navy

*twelve*

Among the Raiders there strongly persisted the feeling that the flyers, in their constant struggle against odds of five to one, were saving Guadalcanal and every American soul on it. It is not surprising that one runs across the following bit of correspondence. On September 21, 1942, Lieutenant Colonel Merritt A. Edson, commander of the First Marine Raider Battalion, wrote to Brigadier General Roy S. Geiger, commanding the First Marine Aircraft Wing and therefore all aircraft on the island:

> There is transmitted herewith, from the officers and men of the First Marine Raider Battalion, to the officers and men of the aviation units under your command, a Japanese flag taken during the fight of 13–14 September.
>
> With this flag we send our congratulations and appreciation for the magnificent work done by the officers and men of our Naval, Army, and Marine Corps units under your command.

To this General Geiger replied:

The Japanese flag captured by your unit during the fight of 13–14 September, has been received at these headquarters, and the sentiments expressed by this gift have been appreciated to the fullest extent by all officers and men of the aviation units at Cactus. [Cactus was the code name for Guadalcanal.] This token of your appreciation and your congratulations for our efforts have made us prouder than ever of our association with the First Marine Raider Battalion. Your actions have been outstanding, and certainly will add a new and glorious page to the history of the Marine Corps. This flag will remain the property of this Wing, and will be turned over for custody to the first Cactus based pilot who shoots down three Japanese planes during one raid.

The extraordinary work of Bauer on October 3, which destroyed not three but five Jap planes, of course gave him the flag, and the same letter from General Geiger established him officially as a Marine Corps ace. But Bauer believed strongly that large scores in air fighting were in part luck and, aside from the skill and pluck of the individual pilot, in large part the result of the combined action of all the flyers who shared the battle, though many of them secured no actual score for themselves. A prize of such spectacular importance as the Japanese flag he refused to keep for himself. He at once donated it to Marine Aircraft Group 23, of which 212 was part, writing, "It is my desire that it be accepted as a Marine Aircraft Group prize and be forwarded to the Marine Corps trophy room, Quantico, Virginia."

A difficulty throughout these days when the war focused on Guadalcanal was that 212 was not based on the island, and only the individual keenness of its pilots in volunteering and the willingness of Bauer to slip them in where he could had enabled them to have any contact with the enemy at all. Standing by at Efate, Espiritu Santo, and other places, their patrols kept watch over huge sections of air and sea, and they could not be spared from these duties. Therefore they lacked the enormous advantage of moving together, as an integrated unit, into Guadalcanal. Thrown in to fill gaps, they fought by fits and starts in small numbers, were withdrawn and sent in again. It should be borne in mind that other squadrons were flying together day after day, practicing as entire teams in the sky, while 212 was fighting in bits and pieces — as though a football team were to break up as an organization and lend out its players to other competitors in little groups. In the meantime, malaria and bad food and the attrition of nerve strength that long-continued war service always entails were weakening the individuals of 212 steadily. Three or four months in such a climate is considered more than ample at a stretch for air fighters in the South Pacific. But

212 had long exceeded this term, and still the most vital period of its fighting lay ahead. October 10 added three more flags, making the squadron's total score 25 to 3, and for each of the pilots involved it was first blood.[1] An enemy task force of cruisers and destroyers escorted by a cloud of Zeros was reported bearing down from the north, and a group of planes from Henderson Field was ordered out to intercept.

Let us follow Huckleberry Watkins for a time. Huck is a quiet young fellow full of Irish, Scotch, Welsh, and the South, with intent eyes that watch the world go by and wait for a place to take hold. Hardly a boy in the squadron was better liked, because Huck was utterly without side or pretense. As one of his chums said, "Just a little old small-town boy, and the best, the very best, all the way through, and no end to him." He was not one to talk of his emotions, but everyone in 212 remembers the day they saw it all in his face. A lot of 212 had arrived at Henderson Field, and a Grumman that had been badly shot up came down streaming smoke to make a forced landing on the fighter strip. But he had too much speed, and he skidded on across the field, across the little Tenaru River,[2] and crashed in a coconut grove. Long before that, Huck Watkins was out of his slit trench and running like mad to get to the spot of the accident. It was one of 212, he thought, and the other boys saw the desperation in his face as he shot past them. He ran across the field, waded and swam the Tenaru in spite of crocodiles in the water always, and on the far side jumped and tore through the barbed-wire entanglements, ripping clothes and skin on the way. But when Huck got there the pilot climbed safely out of the smoking plane, and he was not one of 212 after all. Still, something of the inner Huck had transpired into open view on that day. "It isn't a thing you can talk about and describe. You just had to see how Huck went by on the way to help a friend. You had to see the look of him and the way he went through the barbed wire like tall grass. After that, we knew something about Huck."

Huck Watkins was looking a little farther than some, around the corner of today and into tomorrow, taking notes on the way. "The war changes everything," he said quietly. "It changes the people in uniform and out. The ones at home are in the war too, only they don't know it. Everyone is more vulnerable. The boys are more vulnerable, and so are the gals. And what a lot of trouble that can make!"

This morning of October 10, Huck took off with Major Smith leading, and they went breezing up by the New Georgia Islands. Through a hole in the clouds Huck had his first glimpse of the ships with their white wakes streaming behind them, turned by the distance to motionless little models, a thing done in colored wax set in a shop window. There was nothing above to worry about, and it looked as though the dive bombers that had come out from Henderson Field would get in their deadly work untroubled. There were a dozen Army P-39s along to help the Grummans when the pinches came. Then at the next blink of the eye, the float-Zeros were on them.

It was the old story of buck fever in your first encounter. Even the dogged resolution of a Huck Watkins gave way to trembling nerves and a mist of bewilderment before the brain. In this flat world which most of us inhabit, things happen quietly, slowly, and on our own level. But the streets in the sky run north and south and east and west and up and down hill, all at once, and at the crossings there are fifty ways, not four, to be accounted for. Left, right, before, behind you, above you, comes the danger.

"There were no commands from Smitty. We just started shooting. I remember getting a couple of them in my sights and mashing down on the trigger, and the tracers were flying ahead of their wings, so that I thought I had them — but I didn't. And all at once it seemed certain to me that I would never hit anything. I was no good. They'd wasted their time training me. And it was a rotten feeling. Then while we were all mixing around, like the insides of a cocktail shaker, all at once I was on the tail of a float-Zero and letting him have it. This time I knew. Something ironed out my crooked, jumpy nerves, and I could tell the bullets were whanging right into him.

"It was a queer thing that happened, then. I don't know what the gunfire had done to the Zero, but the pilot of it didn't try to dodge away from me. He acted as though he'd forgotten that the sky is full of holes you can drop a plane through to get away. He just gave up the fight and bailed out. The son of a gun, he didn't have any luck. The plane was all I cared about, not him. But he jumped right into the stream of my tracers. I'm sure they must have hit him, because he didn't open up his parachute all the way. Instead of that, it just seemed to wrap around him as he went down."

Other pilots were getting at the Japs in the air. The P-39s, too slow or too out of position, didn't get into the brawl, but the vicious little Grummans did the job without them. As the Zeros began to be shaken out of the tree, the joy of Major Smith came shouting over the radio: "Jesus Christ, have I got a field day!"

He had reason to shout with excitement, they were doing such a good job, with nobody being hurt. It was all plus and no minus. Still, there was more work and of a different kind to do, for after brushing aside the cloud of Zero interceptors, the next task was to strafe the decks of the cruisers and destroyers so effectively that the dive- and torpedo-bombers could get in their hits without being murdered by anti-aircraft fire. Watkins's target was a destroyer.

"I don't think they felt too good on that destroyer," he said, "because you can tell your misses by the splashes in the water, at a time like that, and there were no splashes as I went over."

Lieutenant Robert Flaherty, who is "Father" or "Pop" to the squadron, was also being blooded on this day. He is a tall boy from Iowa, with a diploma from Gonzaga University in Spokane, Washington, and an excellent scholarship record. He has an amiable, rollicking manner, and sometimes one has to listen closely to find the irony that gives a sharp edge to his words from moment to moment. A strong and clear intelligence, he has the Irish love of banter, and only in a glimmer or a flash one sees that gray-blue light of battle in his eyes as one finds it in all these young air fighters. He had had his troubles in training, landing once with his wheels up, and then a day or two later the landing gear of his fighter collapsed and the plane skidded down the runway on its back. Those accidents coming so close together had shaken his spirit, but he had stuck it out, encouraged by a wise commander. Nearly every pilot has a chance or two of being rubbed out during his training period; nearly all can thank God and good luck for their lives before the happy day comes when they are masters of their planes in all ways and weathers.

Along with the rest of 212, Flaherty had been given his fine points by Bauer, and he gives us a fairly detailed picture of what used to happen when a green pilot first had his mind read by the master pilot, and of those mistakes that green ignorance and eagerness combine to produce.

"The first time I went up and dogfought with Bauer, he was in a trainer SNJ and I was in a Grumman, to find out how an inferior plane could fight against one with superior performance. I pulled an overhead pass on him from about eight hundred feet when I really needed five or six thousand at least for elbow room. Instead of waiting for altitude, I couldn't help fighting him right from takeoff. I should have got up there and started swooping at him the way a hawk does, using the speed of the dives to take me upstairs again after each pass. But he just turned inside me, and after I made that first pass I found myself flattening out on the green of the jungle, and it looked like getting out of there damned quick. But right then my old engine got tired and folded up. It was a pretty near thing, but I managed to make a safe landing. Bauer said I did a damned fool job of fighting but a damned good job of landing.

"So I got into another plane and took off again. This time I put a lot more sky under me, and of course the more sky you have, the better off you are. I began making passes on him. He kept turning inside me and had me completely outmaneuvered. I had the better plane, and I knew something about flying it, but nothing compared with the Coach. When we landed he told me off, point by point, and he certainly could make himself clear. Nobody minded his tough way of talking, though, because it was better to learn through the Coach than through Jap gunfire. And there was nothing personal about him. He was simply comparing you with the man he wanted you to be."

Flaherty went on: "He took me right up in the

SNJ against another fellow and showed me my mistakes one by one and how to remedy them. He showed me just what position to get in when you fight a superior plane: behind, below, and always turning so that when he's shooting at you, you're shooting at him. And always be aggressive; never hang back; get hold of the other fellow in the air and never let go of him until he's dead or gone."

When it came to the pinch, this October 10, those lessons were not wasted. Pop Flaherty was flying wing on Major Smith, and as Smith peeled off on a biplane, a float-Zero came down on the major's tail. The biplane was dropping in smoke and ruin as the Zero dropped on Smith, but before the Zero had an instant to steady himself and make a pass, Flaherty had shot him to pieces. "He simply blew up and went showering down through the sky." At the same moment a float-Zero dropped on Flaherty's tail, only to be shot off it by the next Grumman. And so it went, as fine an exhibition of teamwork as ever was seen over the South Seas.

Then they were in on the Jap warships, strafing. "These cruisers had twin 5-inch anti-aircraft guns. They went boom-boom, shooting together, and threw up balls of flame as big as this room. Coming down at them, strafing, it looked as though I were flying right down the mouth of the gun. I nearly was, because I got a big gash in my cowling. I had a few holes in the tail of my plane, too. But they were .50-caliber, and nobody could explain how *that* happened; but in a big dogfight you have to keep thinking fast to be always sure which is friend and which is enemy."

Cloudy Faulkner, getting his first Jap on this day, had a harder time of it. "As we hit them I saw as many as three at one time going down in flames. I made a pass on a float-Zero, and as I closed in on him he turned into me. I let him have it with a good long burst, and then I had to bank sharply to avoid colliding with him. He was making his pass right through to the end, that fellow was. But perhaps he was already a little sick, because when I looked down a second later he was among those that were dropping in flames."

Faulkner continued: "I'd been scared to death up to that instant, but when I saw that Zero being crossed off the list, it was mighty soothing to me all over. It seemed all at once as though I were just too lucky to be hit. So I got in among the Japs, and they started changing my mind for me. They gave me a good working over. I was making a run on one Zero when another got on my tail and let me have it. As I went up in a climbing left turn I could see the tracers coming at me — what they write in the sky certainly has a lot of meaning; heard them thudding into my plane. As the bullets hit me I could only think of turning over on my back and diving away. I threw the plane over to my left so quick that I did a snap roll, which would have left me in plenty of trouble. But that was where Huck shot the Zero down and most certainly saved my life, because the Jap had me dead to rights.

"Later on I was making a run on a Zero and was just about ready to open fire when he exploded all over the sky. If I'd touched my trigger a second before, I would have claimed that fellow. Which goes to show you that a lot can happen in the air, and how fast.

"We went down to strafe the ships, and I remember that the fire of the smaller anti-aircraft looked like Roman candles, but the big 5-inchers were the scary business. We had a cruiser under us, and we went in on one end of it and out the other with every slug going to town. And as we came out I remember how the shrapnel was falling into the water all around us.

"I saw our bombers come in to do their job on the ships. A dive bomber put a thousand-pounder on the bow of a cruiser, and the big ship lay dead in the water, a mighty pretty thing for American eyes to see. Then a torpedo plane came in and made a perfect hit, but the bad luck was that the torpedoes that day had all been set wrong back at the field, and not a one of them worked!"

Cloudy and all the rest of the Grummans got safely back to Henderson Field, to make it a perfect day, but in the tail of Faulkner's plane there was a hole as big as a washpan made by a 20-mm shell. The little Grumman had flown perfectly in spite of this punishment. "That was the

141

beautiful thing about the Wildcats. They certainly could take it, and they certainly could dish it out, though sometimes you felt you were in a truck when you wanted a racing car."

# VMF-212's Mechanics Build a New Air Force

*thirteen*

★ The Japs were putting continuous pressure on Guadalcanal now, by air, sea, and land. It had been impossible to prevent the arrival of reinforcements on the island, though the Jap ships had to run a bitter gauntlet to come down the alleys from Tokyo. Another flight of Jap planes attacked Guadalcanal's airfield October 11, and again were turned aside, losing a dozen planes, while the pilots of 212 were out over the sea again joining in the attack on cruisers and destroyers still pouring down the Chute into the Solomons.

Over this section of the ocean there was no air opposition after the slaughter of Japanese planes and ships the day before. A torpedo exploded in the side of a cruiser at the same time as a thousand-pound bomb hit the rear gun turret and knocked it into a junk heap. "It certainly stamped that ship down into the water," said Flaherty. "When I went in, there were only three AA (anti-aircraft) guns firing at us, whereas usually it was just like flying down Broadway, there were so many of those gun flashes winking in our eyes. When I strafed, I went right down over the ship, not more than two hundred feet above it. The decks were just covered with men trying to get off the cruiser, and with those six .50-calibers I carved a passage right through the middle of the crowd. I saw the men falling, some of them knocked right over the side of the ship." He added, with a touch of that savagery which sooner or later was bound to appear even in the best of our fighter pilots, "That was about the most fun I ever had. In fact, I was so interested in it that I damned near hit the water."

The Americans lost one plane that day, a torpedo-bomber, but the crew was salvaged. First Lieutenant Robert Stout, one of the most capable leaders and brilliant flyers of 212, was now coming into action, and it is typical of the scattering way in which 212 was brought into the fight, because of multiple other duties, that this outstanding pilot was getting his first chance against enemy planes hardly a month before the recall of the squadron from the South Seas. And again one cannot help wondering what the score would have been if Bauer had been able to fly his crack team against the Japs for a single, continuous period with day after day of sky patrol where action was possible.

A Wyoming lad from the university of that state, big, handsome, casual, with the rambling gait of a range-rider that brought him his nickname of Cowboy, Stout was an utterly unusual combination of humorous relaxation and intense devotion to his work. He became a leader of whom 212 says that if it was possible to find a fight within the circle of the horizon he was sure to get you into it, but he always brought his flyers out safely. Stout had worked eight hours a day to put himself through his years at the university. Then he was with the Bureau of Reclamation with headquarters at Denver. The best days he ever hopes to have will never equal the years up there in the mountains at the head of Green River, among a thousand lakes, with leisure hours to whip the trout streams. His older brother had gone to college like a king but in Cowboy's day fortune was different. He had joined Marine aviation and had had the usual series of troubles and crack-ups until flying sense came to him, as to the others, in one bright, quick day. But the very first Guadalcanal flight he made was one of the saddest experiences of his life.

"We were sent out to give cover to some of our fleet. We knew there'd been a hell of a battle, and we went out there to circle and just see that no Japs came in to strafe.[1] We got out there and found one of our cruisers burning from bow to stern. There were good American destroyers burning, too. Our ships out there, burning to cinders! I flew down low, and while I was making a circle, one of the ships disappeared. The sea is full of little dots, and every dot is a man swimming, and dying, because help doesn't come. Everywhere good fellows going down, and we're up there in damned airplanes and can't do them any good. I look at a group of a dozen and try to

145

pull my eyes away from them, but I can't. And then there are eleven, ten, nine, eight. Every dot that's rubbed off the page is a drowned man, and nothing we can do from up there in the sky. The radios of the ships were silent. If we could have heard something over the air, it might have been better. Finally Higgins boats and other ships got out there to save what was left, but it was a bad day. I never had a worse day than that. I'll tell you what, this business about patriotism and all that seems pretty abstract, just words, just an attitude. But as I circled around over those dead men, because they had to die no matter how they fought to live, it came to me that there *are* big things; it came over me how big they really are."

This was on October 12. The day before, Captain Quilter of 212 had put one flag on the scoreboard, shooting down a Zero, the twenty-sixth count for 212. On October 13 the pounding Japs once more were in the air over Guadalcanal in their ceaseless efforts to incapacitate the field from which the bombers and fighters went up that were blasting the road of the Tokyo Express, by air and sea. Bad days had begun for Guadalcanal and its Marines. Jap pressure was increasing, and our planes were being crippled by the breakdown of parts, or injury from gunfire. And it was at about this time that only five fighters could take to the air, a pitiful force against the swarming Japs. And their bombers were getting hits on the field. The darkest hour was nearing for our air forces at Guadalcanal. And in that unhappy time the mechanics of 212 performed Herculean tasks. In seven days they increased the fighter force, without the arrival of a single new plane, from five to forty-five. They brought junk heaps to life and made them fly again.

This great work was done by men under the command of Gunner Tom Griffis. Back on Efate he and Gunner Edmundson, that mechanical genius, had tossed a coin to see which of them should win the chance to make the trip to Guadalcanal. It was a strange prize that they contested for, since by this time the men had come to the firm conviction that Guadalcanal would be another Wake Island, meaning certain death or capture. The Japanese pounding was so continual and heavy, the American support was so weak and uncertain, that it seemed sure the place must fall, and before long. And yet every man 212 sent up to the island was a volunteer, an eager volunteer, keen to get to the ringside and then into the ring and the battle. They knew that it meant sleeping in the muddy filth of the slit trenches through nights when shells were screeching through the air for hours at a time; it meant short rations, sickness, and daily work to exhaustion. But there is a divine impulsion in brave men to test themselves to the fullest, to lift their uttermost pound of weight, and in this case there was the terrible urgency of friends in need of their help.

Griffis went up to Guadalcanal with a group of fifteen mechanics, and they went to work. "One thing was wonderful about it. Down there in Efate we had to beg, borrow, and steal stuff to do our patching with, but at Henderson Field we were rich in junk. Planes were scattered around in heaps; there were chunks and fragments and bits of everything. We looked at that heap of junk and just laughed, there seemed so much of everything."

Where everyone worked with such devotion it is hard to pick out the best, but Technical Sergeant Lamoureux stood out in all eyes. He was only a boy, twenty or so, but big, strong, distinguished in appearance and bearing. "He just had more brains than most people. He finished junior high school when most boys are just starting, and he got himself into the Marines when he was barely fifteen or sixteen. In four years he had worked himself up to technical sergeant, and in the Marines that means something. He was something, and he looked like something. Let me tell you, if Hollywood ever saw that guy, they'd forget about Clark Gable." As a matter of fact, he is said to be the youngest man ever to make the grade of Marine technical sergeant. Positive, direct, keen, he could carry the men along with him through tremendous efforts. In addition, he was an expert aviation mechanic and full of inspired invention when makeshifts had to be used.

Bombs could not drive these men from their labor. Long before breakfast they were toiling at the injured planes. They came back to swallow some food — hardtack and spoiled coffee, perhaps — then they went back to the job and carried on until twilight had thickened into black night. They staggered back to their camp, blackened by a foul mixture of grease and tropical mud, and fell into their blankets. But in the dark of early morning they were dragging themselves up once more, driven by the deadly necessity to keep those planes flying. Sometimes they dropped their tools and fell asleep under the planes they were working on, so they wouldn't lose an instant of the day's light. These were the men, and this was the way they rejuvenated forty grounded planes in a week and once more enabled the flyers to ward off the steady river of Jap air power that flowed against Henderson Field.

"There were a lot of hard men up there. Some of them had criminal records, some of them were still thieves on Guadalcanal. But they were good fighters. You might say they hated the Japs more than they did the law. All the same, it's wrong to think that our soldiers were all saints and heroes. Some of them had the marrow scared right out of their bones. Some of them went to pieces and had to be shipped out. You'll find them today in hospitals that take care of nerve cases, with their minds gone forever. But most of the blood, the dirt, and the trouble could be washed away, and the Marines who went through Guadalcanal are bigger and better men today than they were before — only mind you, they're pretty hard."

It is not true, however, that on the whole they were inspired by hatred of the Japanese. In war, the enemy is the strange creature on the other side of the hill, monstrous because unseen and hated because he is so feared. Come to handgrips with him, and he's the same spindling little creature that stands in our own ranks. Hate is not the proper inspiration for the fighting man. Hate narrows the eyes and obscures the brain, and the modern soldier needs to have his wits about him every moment. The variety of his dangers, and of the weapons with which he hits back, demands cool calculation at all times. There were outbreaks of blinding rage, of course, for some of the Japanese work in the Solomons was bestial in the extreme. "And it kind of makes you feel sour when you sneak along a jungle trail and come across one of your buddies hung up by the heels with his eyes and tongue gouged out." But it was not the blindness of anger that enabled the handful of flyers and Raiders to receive day after day the impact of overwhelming Japanese numbers and turn them back. Many and many a time the Japs had pushed the Americans to the very cliff's-edge, the extreme brink of the final disaster that would mean swift torment and murder for every man, but the last step was never quite taken, a thin, thin line of Raiders remained in place, and a dwindling handful of fighter pilots kept brushing the sky clean. Hatred was not and never could be the inspiration of such work. There was love of country, but of the kind that keeps the tongue quiet and the hands at work; the air was filled, instead, with the soldier's poetry, infinite floods of rhythmical profanity with the meaning of the words quite forgotten. The cause for which they fought was almost forgotten too in their deep devotion to one another. Perhaps in a more controlling sense than any other, they were aware of war as a game, and the best fighters of all found something to laugh at.

# Darkest Hours

## fourteen

★ One of the darkest of all periods on Guadalcanal was beginning to draw toward its climax now. Repeatedly the Jap bombers broke through the weakening air defense and scored hits on Henderson Field, and ships standing close to shore shelled the field by night. At 11:30 on the morning of October 13, twenty-four bombers and fifteen Zeros came over. Not only was the field hit several times by bombs, but precious aviation gasoline went up in flames. At 3:00 that afternoon, fifteen bombers and ten Zeros were over the field again, one plane going down under the deadly guns of Captain Joe Foss of Squadron 121. But again the field had been damaged. At 1:30 that night, planes dropped flares on the field and shelling commenced from the sea. At 8:00 on the morning of October 14, enemy guns were reported in position on the beach just off the airfield. At 11:45, two flights of bombers came over, radar reporting them too late to let our fighters rise to intercept. At 3:00 in the afternoon, twenty-five aircraft were over Henderson Field, but on this occasion they were so thoroughly intercepted that all were shot down. Still the pressure was

152

kept up despite frightful air losses. And at 9:15 that night, news came which explained the unrelenting enemy attacks. A task force of fourteen ships had been sighted 180 miles from Guadalcanal.

The Jap transports came in two columns of three ships each, surrounded by cruisers and destroyers, all bristling with anti-aircraft guns. But Henderson Field had not been put out of action, and our bombers punished the fleet the moment it was sighted. That night more flares were dropped over the field, and heavy shelling struck it. In the dawn, five enemy ships were reported only twenty miles away, nine more between Savo and Guadalcanal. At six on the morning of October 15, enemy transports were engaged in landing operations between Kokumbona and Doma Reef on the northeast corner of Guadalcanal. Four single-plane attacks were pushed home so gallantly and effectively by our boys that by seven, three of these transports were burning furiously. Two of the covering force of Zeros were shot down, but it was impossible to tell what troops had been landed, or the amount of supplies that had come ashore with them. By eleven that morning, more bombers were over Henderson Field untroubled by any interception, and field artillery was shelling the field constantly.

It was a crescendo of calamity. Here and there the shrinking air force of the Americans struck as it could, but not only had the number of planes dwindled, the shortage of gas was so great that the pilots began to draw rifles from the Raiders and prepare for a last fight on the ground, so sure were they that they would not be able to get into the air. It looked in fact like the end of the long defense of Guadalcanal, which already had endured for more than two months, and no sensible man on the island believed that the Japanese pressure could be endured much longer. Their accumulating forces in the air and on land and sea were far too great to be fought off without immediate reinforcement. Besides, the incessant hammering was wearing down the outnumbered Americans, and the screaming shellfire at night prevented sleep and refreshment. Dark thoughts were turned south toward General MacArthur, the supreme commander, in Australia, by the men of Guadalcanal.[1] But the great sea distances that had to be covered, the overall shortages not only of supplies but of shipping and escort vessels and air protection, were realized and taken into consideration by at least some of our fighting men. On the other hand, two months without succor of any real size or importance seemed a bitterly long time. And obviously the eye of the whole Japanese nation was fixed upon the recapture of the island and its all-important airfield. Tojo seemed ready to pour out his full strength to win back Guadalcanal, but America offered the defending Marines little more than newspaper space.

As a result of the shellings of the last three early mornings, twenty-eight of our planes were destroyed and a dozen more so damaged that they needed major overhauls. It seemed, indeed, that the end of our air power on the little island had come. Yet with the handful of planes that remained, the defenders continued to strike back courageously, not conserving strength to meet Japanese bombing and fighter attacks but sending out, on October 16, no fewer than seven ground attack missions.[2] From three to fifteen fighters and dive bombers strafed and bombed the area of Kokumbona, catching the Japs by hordes in their landing boats and slaughtering them unmercifully. As many as forty of these craft were under attack at one time. In addition, various supply and ammunition dumps were destroyed with 100- and 500-pound bombs, and the whole weight of the blow which the Japanese were preparing was altered and diminished. Those savage little excursions to Kokumbona may have been the salvation of the island.

But other signs of hope were to appear, making October 16 a memorable day in the history of Guadalcanal. The evening before, the old destroyer *McFarland* had come in with a cargo of precious aviation gas, and on the sixteenth, with two scout bombers hovering overhead, a landing barge was being loaded with drums of gasoline.

In the meantime, Admiral John Sidney McCain, commanding all land-based Navy and Marine flyers in the region, had called Bauer to his flagship, the USS *Curtis*, in the harbor at New Caledonia and told him frankly just what the

155

situation was on Guadalcanal. He told of the heavy shellings, the increasing pressure, the number of casualties, the lack of gasoline; he finally told Bauer of the attitude of the men with whom he had been talking during a visit to the island. They thought they were condemned to die, and they had shaken hands with McCain after the fashion of men who were taking a last farewell. In the air, the flyers of Group 23 were exhausted by the good job they had done so long.

Bauer instantly decided to go in with his squadron. He didn't expatiate to his men on the grim conditions that would be found at Guadalcanal, but he let them know that it was the great pinch at last. It seemed in fact work for a suicide squad, but the men of 212 let their commander do the worrying for them. They had now been under his leadership so long, and the affection and faith between him and his pilots were so strong, that he didn't have to ask who wished to go. He knew he could count on every man. The largest number of 212 ever to go into action were assembled on this day. After Bauer came Major Payne and Captain Quilter, then Captain Everton, and Second Lieutenants Sigman and White, Master Sergeant Tex Hamilton — Hamilton bound quickly now for more glory and then for death — Lieutenants King, Stout, Faulkner, Baker, indomitable Huck Watkins, Bastian, Rogers, philosophical Massey, Chamberlain, Flaherty with strange adventures before him, Drury, Freeman, and that young eagle Conger, who now was to prove himself the squadron's outstanding ace.

Altogether in the flight there were nineteen Grumman Wildcats and seven SBD dive bombers. Freeman flew wing on the colonel as they took off from Efate, and his account of the flight serves as well as any. Shortly after the start he found that one of his wing tanks would not transfer gas, and as far as he knew, it would be impossible for the plane to make Guadalcanal without that reserve of fuel. He flew up beside Bauer, motioned to his left tank and shook his head to indicate that it was out. The Coach indicated that one of his own tanks was not delivering, but still he was keeping his place at the head of the flight.

"I figured that if it was good enough for him, it was good enough for me, but I knew it was a mighty long pull up there to Guadalcanal."

By using his fuel pump Freeman managed to get a little gas out of the failing tank for perhaps a minute. Then, as he switched from one tank to the other, the motor would falter and the pilot's heart would fail. That was the fashion in which Freeman struggled through the air toward Henderson Field. The squadron was to split into two parts on arriving over the field, one portion to cover their landing and to strafe the beaches, where from last reports they expected to find the Japs disembarking. The Japs were not, however, along the beaches, and a second order by radio from Bauer was misunderstood by the rest of the squadron. Freeman, for instance, while circling the field, looked up and saw nine bombers flying over it, but he thought they were friendly and heard nothing over his radio to the contrary. Besides, his gas gauge had begun to flicker, which indicated he was nearly out of fuel. He had a feeling also that if there was so little gas on Guadalcanal, the fifty gallons he'd been unable to draw from his left wing tank might be a thing of value. Therefore he landed, and a moment later there were tracers flying about him as he made a dive for a foxhole.

The whole squadron in fact landed in some confusion, but in the meantime a bright new chapter was being written for 212 in the air above their heads by their commander, flying alone against odds of nine to one. For the string of nine bombers were not American. They were old-fashioned Aichi-99 dive bombers, and their target was the unfortunate USS *McFarland* with her invaluable cargo of gasoline for the planes. "The Japs always seemed to know where our ships were. We could fool them with our plane movements pretty often, but the minute any of our ships showed up, we knew that the air would be full of enemy planes in no time."

In fact, the dive bombers came right over the old ship and hit her like a sitting duck. The lighter beside her, loaded with gas, exploded in a huge black cloud, and the rear end was blown out of the *McFarland*, although later she was towed to Tulagi for repairs. By now, however, some measure of retribution was overtaking the dive bombers. Bauer had seen and recognized them and called for his squadron, and when his order was not noticed in the radio confusion, he characteristically started out to execute the mission by himself.

The ground crews and flyers of Henderson Field, who already were cheering wildly because of the arrival of 212, now had a chance to see a masterful bit of fighter-piloting. One after another the colonel overtook and blasted out of the sky no fewer than four of the Japs, and he landed back on the field in a state of high excitement. "Chamberlain, where the hell were you?" he called to the first of his boys he saw. "There was the table all set, and enough for the two of us! The least you could have done was count 'em for me!"

It was that spectacular action of Bauer's that made him a familiar name among the Raiders of Guadalcanal. They had heard of him and of his command before, but October 16 was the dark hour, and in the very midst of it the colonel came in with his men and that brilliant four-ply victory in the air. It was 5:30 in the evening when he went after the Japs. Before dark the word had spread among all who had not been lucky enough to see that engagement, with the four Japanese planes dropping from formation in flames, one after another. That daring and expert work seemed to the Raiders more than merely heroic. Coming in the lean days and in the midst of the aviation-gas famine, it seemed like a token of returning air strength. It seemed above all an omen of better luck to come.

As a matter of fact, more gasoline was flown in. More came by sea, and 212 was able to use its wings continuously for many days in a row. But the sheer brilliancy of the colonel in the air, the eleventh-hour arrival of the squadron, the "American madness" of his singlehanded attack, created new air for the Raiders to breathe. They threw their helmets into the air; they came out of their slit trenches and stinking foxholes to yell and whoop and dance until the startled Japanese, hearing the furor, called off their own attack. They were sure from this outburst of noise that in some mysterious manner the devilish Americans had managed to secure fresh and powerful reinforcements, for men who are about to die are not supposed to be so cheerful about it — not even if they have the pleasure of dying for the Son of Heaven.

There were days when 212 did far more for its country than on October 16, 1942, but this moment was by accident so staged, so set off, so stamped in the minds of the long-enduring Raiders, that it is established as 212's special moment, its bright niche in history.

# The Pressure Continues

## fifteen

★ The last members of Marine Aircraft Group 23, weakened by malaria and combat fatigue, were now free to evacuate Guadalcanal, flying off in air transports, reducing the number of fighter pilots left on the island to fly a patchwork of planes; and 212 had its hands full of work. Even the official account forgets its stilted language and breaks out like a groan to say, "Today was miserable as the enemy continually drove home his bombing attacks. And in this afternoon the enemy field pieces opened again from the hills."

This was "Millimeter Mike," who, day by day in the afternoons, when most of the air raids had ended, made life uncomfortable on Henderson Field with his steady shelling. It was vain for the Marine airmen to scour the hills low down to find the gun emplacement. The smokeless powder left no stain in the air; the flash of the gun was not spotted by daylight; and Millimeter Mike continued to grow into legend as one of the regular thorns in the Marine flesh. It was part of the duty of 212 to locate this perennial evil if they could. But all anyone could claim was that a heavy rain

161

of bombs on probable territory sometimes secured a day or two of silence; and then once again
that solitary voice commenced to speak from a
new part of the hills, harder on the nerves than
a dog howling at midnight.

VMF-212 was nerving itself to try to live up to
the reputation which suddenly had been given it.
"I remember Cowboy Stout holding his head in
his hands and groaning, 'My God, we'd better be
better than good. Have you heard them talk?
They're going nuts about us. They say we're the
best squadron in the world.' " Perhaps it was this
added challenge that helped them in the difficult
days to come.

October 17, right after the Great Day, they set
up camp. Bauer was now in command of the
fighter strip and all its Army, Navy, and Marine
planes. Some from carriers would stay temporarily; others were more permanent. "It meant that
he couldn't give all his time to his squadron. But
we had him with us just the same, and that was
enough to make us feel pretty good." On this day
he had his boys clearing away space in the jungle
so as to give cover and camouflage for the Ready
Tent.

Flaherty said, "Sometimes he only saw things
one way. They were the little things that don't
much matter, but when he got his mind made
up, it was hell for anybody to change it. We were
putting up the big, long Ready Tent, and he said,
'Let's run a ridgepole between the two end poles
to hang up our gear.' I said, 'I've got a piece of

rope here that can serve as a ridgepole and make things nice and tight.' He said, 'No, I think we should put up a pole.' I said, 'I don't think we can get any nails big enough to make it fast. I still think a rope would be better.' He said, 'Well, okay then, we'll put up a pole.'

"I stood there and laughed at him, and he said, 'Pretty hard to make me change my mind, isn't it?' I said, 'I don't know; did you *ever* change it?' He thought that was pretty funny. But we did find a pole that would work, though it cost us an hour of hunting in the woods!"

That night the field was shelled once more from the sea, and again it was proved that a man's nerves can stand almost anything better than shelling.

"You hear a bomb come down squealing like a pig, but it's only that one bomb, and it was dropped from pretty high up in the air. Not so many chances that it will get *you*. I don't mean that it's fun, but you can stand it all right. Now, shelling is different. Say Tojo has dropped some flares to light up his target, and now he has his planes cruising around in the air upstairs to direct the gunfire as the battleships open up. When the big shells land they can gouge out a thirty-foot crater and bucket all that tonnage of rock and soil into the air. It has to come down somewhere, so why not on you? You hear the shell come in, zing-boom-b-r-r! and the thing hits and goes whoom! and the ground shakes under you. That's off to your right. Another one comes along and

163

goes whang, and that's the same distance on your left. Now they've established their bracket, and the next one that comes is sure to have your name and address written all over it. So your diaphragm turns to stone and you stop breathing, and here she comes zooming again and goes crash. And after a while it comes over you, gradually, that you're still alive. You feel buried alive. That's because you haven't been breathing for a while. And by the time you've taken half a breath there's another shell with a label on it cruising in from the sea. You get up in the morning feeling a little gone and spill half the coffee out of your cup, your hand is so unsteady."

So October 18 arrived, the jungle steam began to rise in the air, and in the new Ready Tent, 212 waited for trouble. It came punctually. At eleven the radar picked up the enemy planes, and the telephone rang. Let us hear our calm friend, big and easy-moving Cowboy Stout, talk about that telephone.

"You sit there in the Ready Tent, or maybe you lie down, and you have a newspaper or a magazine, let's say, and everybody is trying to look sleepy and relaxed, because if you see tension in another fellow it builds up the tightness and expectation in everybody else. But a queer thing is that pages hardly ever turn. The boys are just lying there and pretending to read. Then the telephone rings, and every page rattles because hands automatically have jerked. You listen. Your stomach muscles contract, but it's just a bit of routine business, or some damn fool wants to talk to somebody about nothing. And then as you relax, zing! goes the damned telephone again, and this time you hear our man saying, 'How many? How far away?' And right off you know that it's another raid. You grab your helmet and run out for the scramble with that sweat in the palms of your hands and the cold stone in your stomach. Scared? Godalmighty, I'll tell you the truth, *I* used to be plenty scared. But after we had our skipper up there at the field with us for a while, there was a big change. I was there and saw the difference growing day by day until some of the fellows would stroll out singing to the tune of 'The Campbells Are Coming': 'The Jappies are coming, ta da, ta da.' "

Bauer now gave them the word with his usual cheerfulness: "Twenty-four bombers are coming down. They've just pulled out of Bougainville. Be here in about an hour. Operations just called up to say so. I want you to get up there, dodge the Zeros if you can, and get at the bombers. That's your mission; they're the only part of the flight that can hurt Henderson Field. But if you can't dodge the Zeros, turn into them. Make head-on passes. You've got every advantage, doing this. Don't be afraid. Turn right into them and mop them up. Go on, now. Beat it upstairs. You're going to get half a dozen of them today, and every damned one of you is coming home to me again."

The boys went out grinning, even though some

of them felt a little shaky. "What a pity," said Cloudy Faulkner, "that the Coach couldn't have gone along with us! But we knew he was right. He was always ahead of us on every job. What he told us we could do, we felt we surely could."

So on that morning of October 18, two flights were scrambled, Everton and Payne each leading three planes. Payne, instead of trying for altitude where his flight would be safer from the Zeros in the upper sky, ignored them and went for the bombers at lower elevation and forced them to jettison their cargoes before they reached their target. He got a bomber on his first pass. Then, as the bomber formation fled away toward Tulagi, he started making passes on a bomber that lagged behind, drew no fire, finally, from the rear gunner, and moved right in until the bomber started the long downhill glide, smoking, then flaming into the sea. Two more flags for the scoreboard of 212 from Beanie Payne.

Faulkner was with Payne's flight that day and with him dodged the Zeros to get at the bombers.

"Beanie rolled into an overhead pass on the formation. The fellow behind him did the same. When it came to my turn, I'd lost a good position and made a poor pass. It was so poor I didn't even bring my guns to bear on a Jap. But I saw Beanie get one, and there was also Jack Conger's bomber exploding right in the middle of the formation.

"This was as the bombers were coming into Guadalcanal. I cut across to get into position as they came out, and I was in perfect position when they came by, so I made a high-side pass on the tail bomber and let him have it right at the root of the left wing. Probably the pilot was killed, because the plane nosed right over and went straight down. Other Grummans were chopping the bombers down. I came up from below and let the new tail plane have it in the belly. Just as I was hitting him, two of the bombers dropped their bombs right in my face. They were lightening up to get away. It made me mad to be cheated; but when I closed in again, I was out of ammunition. On my way home a Zero caught me and plastered me. I hid in a cloud, and when I reached the field there were plenty of holes in my plane. One of them was through the cockpit.

"It was queer what could happen to you in the air from bullets and still you'd get home. The armor helped a lot. I've counted eight dents in the armor plate behind my seat after a single flight. Any one of them would have ended things for me. I saw Huck Watkins come down with a plane so badly shot up that the mechanics pushed it out into the weeds and left it there."

Besides Payne's, there was Everton's flight in the air going great guns. He had gone up to about twenty-six thousand feet, climbing straight on when Payne turned off at the bombers so that he could make a second attack on the same target. But as Everton started his attack he saw that he would be sucked in behind the Mitsubishis into their slipstream of bullets. Instead of carrying on, he rose into the formation of Zeros above the bombers, for up there the Jap fighters were drifting along doing slow rolls. "Which shows how terribly stupid they can be; we never do any tricks in the air at all. When I got in among them I hoped to take enough of their attention so that they couldn't break up our attack below. They were all over the sky. One of them turned back into me from above, and it seemed to me that I could feel the bullets from all six of my guns smashing into him. He exploded; I flew through smoke and flames and bits of shattered plane. The Jap pilot fell, dead of course. I saw him splash in the sea. All that was soundless. Outside of the roar of your own motor and your own guns, the sky is always silent. But there's something always coming in over your radio. When 212 was fighting you'd hear the boys saying, 'I got another of the sons of bitches. . . . There's a Zero on your tail, Jack!' and a lot of other language that paper wouldn't hold. And all the time down there on the field would be the Coach straining to see every move through his glasses. And as the Japs began to streak down out of the air, the listeners on the ground radios who were also watching began to go crazy and jump up and down worse than you ever saw people at a football game when the home team comes from behind and wins the fight."

Everton got a second plane that day, by rare luck and flying, finding himself above one of the Zeros and diving on it from the rear. He killed the pilot and hit the gas tank. One instant of contact and the Jap was going down in flames, and Everton could see a broken part of the cockpit where the bullets had hit it. This victim dropped in the mountains at the northern tip of the island.

Jack Conger was up there with Doc Everton — as usual, wild with excitement as he tried for the kill. When he saw his flight leader turn uphill to ward off the Zeros, Jack went in at the Mitsubishis. He made a long run, once more opening fire from too great a distance. But as he closed in he held down the trigger for a long burst — seconds of continuous heavy fire. "I was practically right behind him, and gee, nothing happened, and yet it seemed to me that my tracers were carving him apart." An instant later he had Everton's experience. The Zero, apparently unscathed, without smoking or giving any outward sign, blew up right in his face. He dived to avoid the flying fragments, but Bastian on his wing flew through the cloud of ruin.

Conger continued: "I was excited, and that doesn't pay. I started making passes without getting enough altitude — three or four short runs, but still I couldn't get another of them. I remember I was out over the sea when a Zero came down from nowhere, making a head-on pass at me. I had quite a lot of speed from my last pass, and I was making a gradual climb, while he was making a gradual dive. He opened up. I saw the winking of his guns — you never quite get used to seeing them blink in your face like that — but

I held on for a second until I thought I had him right. Then I gave him a three-second burst, and he smoked, fell off on one wing, and went right in."

As the others said, "Some men simply are not made for fighter pilots; they have to be born that way and then trained." But Conger never was in the air without that dash, that electric overplus.

# Pop Flaherty Makes It Back

## sixteen

The colonel had asked for six flags for the scoreboard that day, and 212 already had furnished seven, but still the scoring was not completed. Pop Flaherty was up there and ready to do business.

"I went out to get my plane, and somebody else already had taken it. I went running up and down the line, and I came across this old Grumman, older than the oldest plane on the field and just about broken to pieces. But I had to get up there in the air. The plane captain said, 'You're welcome to it. Anytime anybody takes it up, something goes wrong, but today I think I've got it fixed.' I said that I'd take it, and he said, 'I sure hope you get along all right. Nobody else has!' "

With this unpropitious start — planes, like ships, can build up a reputation for good or bad luck — Flaherty climbed into the air and joined Everton, the last man in his flight. He was with them when they made their interceptions fifteen miles up the channel. It was Pop who first saw the Zeros overhead, and as his position was wrong for an attack on the Mitsubishis, he turned up to meet the fighters. One of them came right downstairs to him. It seemed to Flaherty that he had the fellow boresighted, but his bullets apparently accomplished nothing. He scooted on past the Zero, but when he turned his head he could see the Jap continuing that headlong pass, not smoking, not flaming, simply making a long, perfect pass that wound up in a little bright flash, far below, as he entered the sea.

"I came back and flew right up the tail of another Zero. I was right dead behind him and inside three hundred yards. You couldn't ask for anything much nicer than that, but when I squeezed the trigger nothing happened. I let go of everything, reached down, and recharged my guns. Only one of them worked. I remembered what the plane captain had said about things going wrong. The first glimpse of my tracers going by, and that Zero got out of there." That was the sad story for the little snub-nosed Grumman Wildcats over and over again. When a Zero wanted to avoid battle, it could be away like a bird from a tree.

There were few Zeros left by this time, so Father Flaherty went after the Mitsubishis. But still, whenever he started to make a pass, the Zeros would come down, and as he rose to meet them head-on, his pass was spoiled. He had pulled out of battle and fooled with the guns until four of them would work. He was about fifty miles away from Guadalcanal toward the Russell Islands, now. Here he noticed that his engine was smoking, but before he could make out the reason, a

Zero made a sideswipe at him, and as it turned he got on its tail. "And that one too burned all the way down to the sea."

Now that he had time to look things over, Pop realized what was wrong. He was down to about nine thousand feet, but he'd left his plane in high blower (supercharger) with full throttle. He shifted his blower to low, cut down on the throttle, and started for home, because that is where a flyer wants to be after an engine has smoked. He was paying no attention to the Japs when the first thing he knew, tracers were whizzing past him and he found two Zeros riding his tail, taking turns in occupying the best position for shooting him down. They used their light-caliber machine guns until the tracers were on him, and then they shifted to their 20-mm cannon, "which knocks you all apart if it gets in a solid hit."

Flaherty had dropped down until he was just a few feet above the water, which makes it difficult or impossible for enemy aircraft to make a sustained diving pass of the usual pattern.

"When I saw the light stuff coming by, I'd skid to the side, and they couldn't turn because they were too close to the water to bank. So far as I know, they never hit me. But now my engine definitely pooped out. I paid no attention to the Japs but worked on my landing. You know what's going to happen when a fighter plane hits the water. There's going to be a heavy impact, and your head, no matter how hard you brace back, is going to be snapped forward. That's one reason

173

why the gunsights are padded with rubber.

"I flattened out, and I suppose that I coasted about half a mile before I hit water. Just as I'd expected, my head snapped forward and hit the rubber of the gunsight, and I found out just what the rubber meant, which was about nothing. When I came to, I had a gash over both eyes. I must have worked with my hands before my brain was clear, because my safety belt had been unfastened and I was floating there in the ocean."

Exactly the same thing had happened to Drury in a similar case; the disciplined instinct seems in part to take care of the trained fighter even when his consciousness is under a cloud.

"I hadn't inflated my life jacket," Flaherty continued. "In fact, I wanted to get under water because I was sure the Zeros would strafe me, but then I saw one of them come over in a slow roll, which is one way of thumbing your nose at the other fellow. The guy may have been out of ammunition, or maybe he was just playing fair.

"I couldn't inflate my lifeboat, but the jacket worked all right. I was just off Savo Island, and I didn't know who was on it. There might be Japs, for all I knew. But it's hard to stay in the sea and not have some place to go, so I started swimming for Savo. It was about two in the afternoon, and the day had turned off bright and hot. Savo looked like nothing but a little green hill stuck there right in the middle of the sea without any fringe of beach around it, so far as I could tell.

"I saw two boats start off from the island, so I got my pistol out. I couldn't see very well because my eyes were full of blood and closing rapidly. However, the pistol was better than dropping into the hands of the Japs. But as the boats came near me I could hear the talk and knew they were natives. Of course, I couldn't tell whether they were friendly, so I kept ready with the pistol. But when they came up they didn't pay any attention to the gun, so I decided that they must be friendly.

"They wanted me to climb in, but I couldn't haul myself out of the sea into a little two-man canoe without tipping everybody out, so I hung on behind till another boat arrived. I was watching a couple of sharks playing around near me while we waited. These natives, by the way, are deadly afraid of sharks. In fact, they're shark worshipers, I understand. If that's the case, that day their prayers worked, because the sharks didn't try to take a chunk out of me.

"They held their canoes together, and I came in over the end. Then they took me ashore and bathed me in fresh water and gave me a sarong. The chief moved out of his place and let me live there. Maybe all this was because they knew I was an American, and because they'd been well rewarded when they helped others of our men. But I think it was because they were just naturally friendly. Probably they would have done the same for a Jap or anybody in trouble.

"They took good care of me. They washed the salt water out of my clothes and gave me some tea, and finally they found an old bottle of benzoin and put some of that on my eyes, because both of them were so nearly closed that all I could see were some fuzzy shadows. After that, they got me to bed.

"I still didn't know whether there were any Japs around, but one of them spoke a little English, and through him I had a man posted on the beach and another on guard at the door.

"I remember sleeping cool and fairly comfortable until the pain in my head woke me up, and there was a native sitting fanning me. He'd been doing it all night.

"The next day I explored to the other end of the island and back again, but all I saw was an old bombed Jap landing boat. I didn't know how I could tell the world about where I was, but there was a good-sized mirror in my survival kit, and I thought that I might be able to signal with that. Just flashing a mirror is a distress signal in the Navy.

"The second day a B-17 came along, and I did my flashing. But the Flying Fortresses are Army, not Navy, and so they answered my distress signal by opening up with their guns. I mean, that's what it looked like to me, and I was pretty sore about it. An American chunk of lead doesn't taste any better than one from a Jap machine gun.

"That evening a couple of Navy dive bombers came over, and I started flashing at them. The first one went straight on, and so did the second, but just as he was at the edge of the sky and disappearing, that second one turned around and came back. He had seen my red baseball cap when I waved at him. Now he gave me the high sign with one hand and went off for help. But about this time my old roommate Sparrow had had some tough luck with the two amphibians on Guadalcanal, and both of the Ducks were out of commission, so I couldn't be fetched in by air.

"The natives were loading some of their big war canoes with fruit to paddle through the islands to trade, and they wanted to get to Tulagi, just across the strait from Guadalcanal, but couldn't buck the current, so they took me with them and went around behind the island, ten men in two war canoes, and another little canoe with one watermelon in it. They touched at a few islands and traded with the other tribes, and that night we touched on the north shore of Florida Island. That meant I had to go the rest of the way on foot, without shoes, crossing over the mountains, but I made out pretty well by stuffing rags into my heavy socks."

Flaherty crossed over to a lagoon in which was lying the destroyer *McFarland*, which had had an end blown off by the Japs. It had been camouflaged so that at a short distance it practically disappeared from the eye. He got on board in time for ten o'clock coffee, a ragged tramp with a horribly gashed and swollen face, but the crew were not too surprised to have a Marine flyer appear out of nothingness. A legend had grown up about their indestructibility. A Marine line officer has said to me, "You could see our planes shot down now and then, but it was hard for the Japs to kill the fighter pilots. The sea wouldn't drown them, and when they hit the ground they just bounced and came back for more."

The destroyer's men delivered Flaherty to Tulagi, well scrubbed and newly clad, and that night he stayed in the old governor's mansion with a chance to rediscover how whiskey tasted and to shave the beard from his face. Next morning he was delivered, along with five hundred barrels of gasoline, to Henderson Field, a worn and haggard young officer extremely glad to be alive.

A jeep carried him up from the tender. "The Coach came running out and grabbed me, but the first thing he shouted while he was still at a distance was, 'Hello, Father, how many did you get?' "

For the score was the thing, the war was the thing, in the mind of Bauer, and the men of his squadron were building his pride in them bigger and bigger every day. He sent Pop Flaherty back to Efate to recuperate. "Go down there and get all rested up," he said, "and when you come back here, you're going to be an ace the first time you get into the air."

But poor Flaherty had made his last flight as a member of 212. He remembered getting on board the ambulance plane, crowded with wounded, and at a place on the walkway between two gasoline tanks he came upon Massey and Bastian. "They were asleep, as usual, but I thought they might be glad to see me because I'd been missing for a week, so I woke them up. Bas seemed pretty happy to have me back, but Massey never said what anyone expected. He said, 'Dammit, Pop, I thought you were lost. Now I owe you that fifty dollars all over again.' After that, we found some medicinal brandy on that plane and made a good trip out of it."

A while later Flaherty got down to Australia by air and from there to a recuperation camp in New Caledonia, where the pilots from Guadalcanal rested up. "We used to call it Camp Despair, because all the time the other boys were up there doing something and we were so far away." And 212 was evacuated from Guadalcanal before he could return.

# More Dogfights — Everton Scores Again

## seventeen

★ The air had been far from still over "the Canal" while Flaherty was away. On October 18 no fewer than thirteen Zeros and eight bombers had been shaken out of the sky, but still the Japs came back for more.

October 19 was a grim day for the squadron, because a savagely displeased Colonel Bauer spoke his mind. Let us have the story in the words of Freeman.

"Quilter led our flight up, and fifteen Zeros jumped us; there were eight of us. I remember firing as I climbed, and the recoil of the guns kept kicking me back. I looked across and saw a Zero slow-rolling on the tail of one of the boys. Being on the low side of our formation, I crossed over beneath and climbed up to get action. There were more Zeros hanging up there on their sides, and I remember a pair close together, waiting on their props. When I fell off in my climb, they dived on my tail. I saw everybody diving out, so I did the same thing. I kept on going down and headed for a cloud bank on the south side of the island, and by that time I'd lost too much altitude to do any fighting worth while. I found Huck Watkins and joined up on him and suggested that we go back and take another crack at the Zeros, but he signaled that he didn't have any guns.

"We just went back and landed. I felt rotten because it looked as though we'd just run away from danger, and certainly it was not the way the Coach had taught us to act in the air. It wasn't my own idea of how to fight either, and I kept thinking about the ground troops who couldn't pull out and run from odds even if they wanted to.

"After every flight we had to go to the colonel and tell him everything we'd seen and done. I was one of the last to come into the tent, and he said, 'Did you stay and fight?' It made me sick, but I had to say, 'No, Colonel.' Then he said, 'You boys must be awfully proud of yourselves for this day's work.' He was so mad that he was boiling. There was still a theory that in the air a pilot should only fight when he saw some advantage, but the colonel said that anything that wore a red dot on it was enemy and must be fought with. After that, he walked to his tent right through our Ready Room and didn't say a word to anyone, except to throw one sentence over his shoulder: 'If you boys don't want to fight, I'm going to start weeding you out and sending you home.'

"If other men had talked like that, it would have made you sour; inside, you would have been telling them to go to hell. But from the colonel it was talk that made us feel pretty rotten. His opinion meant more to me than any medal the president could pin on me."

Altogether it was a black day for 212, and it included a shrapnel wound in the shoulder that incapacitated unlucky Chamberlain. The score for the squadron was now forty-one enemy planes shot down. Far less than a month remained for action, and it is curious to note that, splendid as the record was for 212, it still was not the near-perfect organization Bauer at last was to make it. On October 19 his men still were not completely in hand, but before the end of the month they made the ideal team of which every air commander dreams. His anger in fact bore immediate fruit, as it had to do with men who dreaded his displeasure far more than they feared Japanese bullets.

October 20 was as full of glory as the preceding day had been of unhappiness. Twelve bombers and twenty Zeros were coming in, and Bauer could put up hardly a third of that number from his fighter strip. We follow Freeman into the sky. With King and Massey, after taking off, Freeman was unable to find the rest of their flight — one more indication of the uncertainties of air battle, where the sky is like a magician's black cabinet and whole armadas vanish or appear in a breathing space. So the three from 212 joined up and went toward Tulagi, climbing for altitude. "If we had missed the Japs when they made their pass at the field, we figured we would get a whack at them as they were pulling out for home. When they showed up, we had altitude on them, but they were about five miles away, and we had to use up our altitude to get in among them. Altitude or not, we were still mad from what the colonel had said the day before, and we went right into them. Massey went into the bombers and got one of them; King and I took over the Zeros. They were everywhere. The Grummans were too slow, and the Japs rose away from us like bubbles going up through water; then they dropped back, making fighting passes on us. I lost sight of King. It was a great day for him; he got two Zeros, but I was in a sky full of Japs. They were everywhere, like birds, all taking a peck at me. While I was shooting at one, two more were coming in on my tail. I was kicking the plane around as hard and fast as I could to make myself as poor a target as possible."

Freeman continued: "I dove into a cloud and came out of it right on the tail of a Zero, but he was almost out of range. When I tried to close in, he pulled away from me just like a train from a station. Then I was coming through the overcast with a score of nothing and only ten gallons left. Besides, I was lost. But I found myself on a map I had in my pocket, and I flew in low over the water, because it's hard to see a plane against the color of the ocean. I was the last to land and got the bad news that King had been shot down. When I walked into the Ready Tent the colonel said, 'Where have you been?' I said I'd been fighting Zeros but I hadn't snagged a single one of them. 'But are you afraid of them, now?' he asked. I said I figured I could handle them, and that pleased him just as much as though I'd brought down three of them. He slapped me on the shoulder and said that was what he liked to hear. It made me feel mighty good; it was better than getting a medal, believe me, when the colonel said the good word."

Everton had been up there at work among the scattering, slow drift of clouds that day. Like a good general, Bauer had held him and his division of fighters in reserve, and they stood by at the Ready Tent, waiting for orders to scramble. Far away among the clouds they now and then saw little drifts of planes fighting, like a whirl of leaves. They could hear the dogfighting, but they caught only broken glimpses of it. And that was hard on them, because they had become so welded together for the battle, and were so moved by that deep sense of comradeship which comes to a fighting man only, that when one of them was fighting in the air, every one of the rest yearned to be with him.

They got their signal to scramble, and Everton, as flight leader, took up five to twenty-six thousand feet before engine trouble sent one of them back to the field. Four planes therefore made up the fighting unit as Everton counted eighteen bombers and six Zeros coming south. The odds were six to one, but that was nothing unusual.

184

He simply maneuvered into position for attack and went at them. On his first pass he started a bomber smoking badly. It meant that the Mitsubishi never would get home, but since it did not go down on the spot, Everton could not claim it.

"I made my pass on the bomber, went under him, climbed up again, and while I was doing a wingover I saw fifteen more Zeros, a whole cloud of them."

That was how Tojo kept producing them out of the dark cabinet of the sky, for he was flinging in men and machines recklessly in those days, confident of victory soon, victory now, and the frightened Americans driven forever out of the Pacific.

"Six to one," continued Everton, "was not so bad, but this new flight of Zeros thickened the soup a good deal. However, the idea in 212 was to stay and fight it out no matter how many came over, so we stayed. It's hard to straighten out a fight, even when I try to remember every detail. I recall asking over my radio for a little help, but the reserve planes were all in action, and nothing could reinforce us. After that, it was too fast for talk. The Zeros were everywhere, taking punches at me. One went down smoking, another dropped in flames, but the rest kept coming at me.

"There was a moment when I had one ahead of me, one on each side, and one sliding in from above. I pulled my nose up and flew right at him till he lost his nerve and shoved off. When I was out of that trap I saw a Zero below me, just puttering around and having a good time all by himself. It was a fine feeling to look at a Zero from above, so I went on down there to introduce myself. I dove and was just on his tail, with the range closing and my finger on the trigger ready to fire a burst, when another Zero only seventy or eighty yards behind began to throw stones at me. I heard the small-caliber machine-gun bullets hitting on my armor plate; then my plane was shaken by a 20-mm shell.

"Over my right shoulder I looked back at the Jap and saw all his guns winking red fire and the pilot leaning eagerly over his sights. At the same time, two of his 20-mm shells smashed into my cockpit, and the shrapnel from the bursting shells hit me in the right side and knocked my leg off the rudder, which caused my plane to roll over on its back and start spinning. First thing I really knew about being hit was that I couldn't move my leg back to the rudder pedal; the next idea that came to me was that the plane should be allowed to spin so that the Jap would think I was going down, out of control and dead.

"I pulled out of the spin at about nineteen thousand. I'd met the Jap at around twenty-five thousand, and the Grummans were pretty slow in the higher levels. Once I roused up a Zero at thirty thousand, and he rose right up into the sky so that I couldn't even stay with him. I had a chance to think a little about my wounds, now. Shrapnel had torn up my right thigh. Two pieces had driven down into the muscle; another fragment had opened a surface gash. There was not much bleeding, and my leg was numb, not painful.

"The flying was not so good. I had to lift my leg with my hand and put it on the rudder pedal. So I called the field and said I was coming in for an immediate forced landing. Pretty soon they called me back and told me to wait. I made another circle of the field and dropped my wheels and flaps. Once more they called to me to wait. They said, 'You can't land here.' I simply said, 'The hell I can't!' And by that time I was on the deck.

"I don't know why they warned me off. I didn't see any enemy planes around. And it still makes me mad to think of that voice telling me that I couldn't land there, when I was pretty fortunate to be able to get down anywhere without crashing.

"My plane was junk when I got it down. They stripped off a few parts they could use, but the rest of it just went on the pile. The fragments of shrapnel are very sharp, and they slash through the thin metal of a plane like a razor through paper."

Everton had to be evacuated on account of his wounds, and this meant that 212 lost a valued flight leader. He had the fine record of four bombers and four Zeros shot down, besides too many smoking probables to mention, but his worth to 212 had been not only as a fighter but as a skillful and daring commander. Cowboy Stout was able to take his place leading a flight.

On this memorable day of October 20, Huck Watkins got a bomber for himself. But Watkins doesn't remember details and prefers to laugh at air oddities and minimize his fine performance throughout.

The day's total for 212 was eight, of which three were bombers, and the squadron score now had climbed to a total of forty-nine. Stout scored a double that day, like Everton and King. Stout had had a great stroke of doubt and conscience when he saw his friend Everton plunge up among the overmastering swarm of Zeros and wondered whether or not he should follow. But the main objective was bombers, always, and Cowboy, unable to get altitude, dove right in on one. When he could get at it in no other way, he went at the tail, regardless of the tail gunner and wondering every moment if a call would come from Everton. "It seemed to me that a little machine gun in the tail of a bomber didn't mean much, but the Jap in the rear of that plane knew how to do his stuff. He sure aerated my Grumman for me. Then I saw pieces flying out of the bomber. It smoked, fell away out of the formation, and went wobbling down."

Cowboy pulled up for another pass and saw Rogers flattening out a little under the bombers; and then he saw a Zero dropping right down on Rogers from above and behind. It looked like plain murder, and Cowboy went zooming down to prevent it. This was first contact for Rogers, who said, "The track was bent on my plane so that I couldn't close the hood, and it was getting pretty cold up there in shirtsleeves, and with the wind blowing me to ice. It must have been below zero, but I knew I couldn't go back just because of an unfastened hood. I knew the Coach wouldn't appreciate that. I had dived at the bombers and came up under them, firing at their bellies until they opened their bomb bays and dropped their bombs — almost as though they were trying to hit me, though actually they were just lightening themselves to get away from there. Somehow I rolled over on my back and didn't see the Zero fasten on to me until Cowboy came whooping down and shot him off my tail — off my belly, I should say. He got that Zero bore-sighted and simply blew him to pieces. When I got back to the field, Cowboy came running up and asked if I were all right. As a matter of fact, my plane hadn't even been hit."

But one more rescue had been performed to weld the squadron closer together, and when a man knows that friends will do all they can to protect him, he is constantly more fearless in flying in the face of danger. These boys were reaching the point when they no longer would count odds or think of turning back.

# Tex Hamilton's Last Flight

*eighteen*

★ The next day, October 21, saw the score of 212 increased by five counts to fifty-four. But still, the day was almost the blackest in the history of the squadron.

The night before had been reasonably quiet except for the monotonously falling shells of "Millimeter Mike" from the hills; and the next morning at the usual time Tojo's boys came over in a beautiful flight of bombers with the cloud of little Zeros up above, clustering in the eye of the sun. Beanie Payne led up a flight consisting of Bastian, Conger, Drury, and Tex Hamilton. A Zero came almost head-on at the flight leader, and Payne swung to a 45-degree bearing on him, opening up on him with a quartering burst as he went by. Payne turned to follow up the attack, feeling that he had not hit the Jap at all — only to see him streaking down in smoke, and then in flames.

Head-on attacks seemed to be the fashion with the Japs that day. They tried big Drury next, and the Zero might as well have charged a mountain. The American closed straight in on him, with an unwavering run and a heavy burst of fire. At the

190

last instant the Jap flinched aside with a flash of flame at the leading edge of his left wing, close to the fuselage. That was where the gas tanks were located, and one more Zero went down, leaving a swiftly drawn exclamation mark of smoke against the sky.

Another passed in front of Drury an instant later, and to get a shot at it, Drury pulled up until he was in almost a complete stall position, with the plane shaking. As he caught the Jap in his sights at last, he put in a long sustained burst and from that sharp angle saw the tracers driving straight home. The Zero fell away and started down, smoking, with Drury following to make sure of the kill. "I saw his helmet fly out, then a lot of white stuff — maybe paper, I don't know. At any rate, he was gone in smoke. I pulled up, and by the time I was back up there I had the whole sky to myself except for one American parachute dropping slowly through the air. The man under it was Tex Hamilton, hanging helplessly in the shrouds — perhaps already killed by gunfire, as he did not wave to me as I repeatedly passed by him. Anyway, I covered him all the way down and marked the spot in the jungle where he landed. I circled after he disappeared, but I got no signals from him, and then I had to come home, short on gas."

It was a loss from which it was not easy to recover. Marine Gunner Henry B. Hamilton was a veteran who'd come in as an enlisted man and had been seven years in the air, not a single hour of it wasted on his cool and intelligent brain. Except for Bauer himself, there was hardly a finer flyer in 212 than Hamilton. He had been a special scourge to the heavy bombers, and he led the entire squadron, with five of them shot down. He had two Zeros to his credit as well. "He was a big fellow, and he didn't say much, but when he spoke up, he was the sort of man that everybody listened to. I think the colonel had special confidence in him. He was the first man to land on the Efate fighter strip, and he was first in a lot of other ways. Because he had come up through the ranks, the ground force had a special affection for him. He was their hero. They felt that on an equal basis he could outfly and outshoot anybody except Bauer. The ground crew had its own way of judging the pilots, and perhaps they were right. They felt that Moon Drury was about the hottest damn thing in the air next to Tex, and maybe he was. They liked the go-to-hell ways of Drury in a plane, and they appreciated the easy style of Hamilton. His landings were so smooth that you didn't have to ask who was handling the plane."

This was the day also of the last wild adventure of Bastian in the air over Guadalcanal, when death missed him by a hairsbreadth as he went to the rescue of his chum Conger. Conger told the story best.

"Huckleberry, Bas, Drury, and I were pretty close; we were thicker than poured concrete. I want to tell you about the time when Bas came out of nowhere and saved my skin. That day I was lost from the rest of the fellows. I looked around, and there was nothing I could see between me and the sun, but down below I saw a Zero and dropped on him and followed him from twenty thousand down to eleven thousand. I got in a couple of good bursts on him, but he wouldn't drop, so we got into a dogfight. There were a lot of big clouds down there, and they formed a sort of arena like a bullring for us to fight in. Then tracers began to go by me from behind, and when I looked back there were two more Zeros sitting on my tail and closing their range. It turned into a general mix-up, each fellow trying to get in a burst and with me doing a lot of evasive action between shooting chances.

"Then along comes a Grumman, and I was mighty glad to see it, and in that Grumman there was sitting nobody else but Bastian. I gave him a big old wave with my hand, like that. The same time, I glanced back behind his plane and saw two more Zeros just coming into boresight range, right on him. I pressed my throat-mike button and yelled, 'Look out, Bas! Two Zeros right on your tail!' But evidently my mike had a bad connection, and he didn't hear me.

"So I saw him sitting there. I was sick, and yet at the same time I was saying, 'I'm glad I'm not in his shoes!' And then, slam! he did a cross right under me, and there were the two extra Zeros hanging right on *my* tail with *me* boresighted. Yes, just as I was thinking, 'Poor Bas!' he goes zip, right under my tail. Of course, he didn't have any idea that he was hanging on me, but it was a great joke in the squadron after that. It tickled the colonel almost to death; he never got tired of laughing at it.

"They peppered me, all right, and let a lot of light into my plane, but I did a flip-over and got out of there. But there were Zeros climbing all over us, six of them to the two of us. I finally managed to get one of them really lined up and put a good burst into him. He fell off into a cloud, and that left only five. A second later there were only four, because Bas kept shooting them off my tail and I kept knocking them off his.

"But then in a moment I was all alone there in that amphitheater of the clouds, with Bas gone clear out of sight and a couple of the Zeros sitting on my tail again. So I dove into a cloud. I was pretty short on ammunition, but I stuck my nose back out after a minute to see what I could do for Bas.

"He wasn't in sight; there wasn't any Bas around at all. It threw a scare into me. He'd come down to help me, and what had I done for him? I dove down through the clouds and out over the jungle and spy-hopped around over the trees, trying to see any signs where a plane might have crashed and burned, but I couldn't see anything, and I began to feel a little better.

"I came back to the field and landed a plane that was another addition to the junk heap, and the first man I see is a big fellow all over red with blood. He comes at me waving his arms and yelling, and that's Bas. I was sure relieved, because the noise he made gave me an idea that he wasn't too badly wounded. Matter of fact, while he was dogfighting, a Jap bullet had cut across the back of his neck. He swears he could see the bullet coming but couldn't get out of the way; I guess he means he could see the line of tracers flying through. Anyway, that bullet cut a groove across the back of his neck that you could lay a pencil in and just missed a vertebra. But still he kept on fighting, because he wouldn't let me down, until finally I seemed to disappear. Then he did just what I'd done. He flew down through the clouds and searched over the jungle for me. When he got low on gas he hopped back to the field, and they tried to get him to a doctor. But he knocked them out of the way and ran around calling for me. He kept saying, 'Where's Jack? He's got to be here. He's *got* to show up!' So pretty soon I came down out of the sky, and that was that. We were both mighty relieved."

And Conger concluded: "But the wound was so bad that Bas had to be sent back to Efate to recuperate, and that spoiled his chance to build up a big score. When he let them stitch up his neck, he couldn't move his head. But if he'd had his chance, he would have been an ace, quick. He knew all the answers, up there."

On October 22 there was only one alert, and when the Japs came over they were turned back with the loss of four planes. One of them went to the credit of White, of 212. "Oxygen at high altitudes made Whitey sick, but he was as game a flyer as you could find. He was a fellow who never wasted a word. Sometimes he was so quiet that he seemed almost sullen, and he'd pass out no answers. But he was a real man. We called him Sambo. He was good-looking, clean-cut, stocky. He'd been a fine football player, and he was plenty rugged; drinks never climbed up to his brain. He and Cowboy and Massey were a poker team, and they were always aiming at a hundred-dollar night. Sambo handled a lot of low-altitude patrols, and they're dangerous because the enemy always had the advantage of being on top. But this day when the dive bombers tried to get at the ships, Whitey went out there to shield them, and that was when he got his plane."

The night that followed was quiet, and this was a blessed relief to the boys of 212. By this time the colonel had grown profoundly worried about their condition. They had been far, far too long in the tropics. Nearly every man was riddled with malarial fever, and the chilly shakes were no help to a man who was trying to make a smooth pass at one of Tojo's boys. Only the desperate necessity of defending Henderson Field, that northernmost defense against the Japs, made Bauer keep his team in action when his lads were losing a pound a day through illness, the strain of constant fighting and patrolling, and the wretched rations. Few of 212 were untouched by digestive troubles, combined with malaria.

It was this combination that almost killed their brilliant flight leader, Major Payne. He was up at twenty-seven thousand feet, a thoroughly sick man belching into his oxygen mask. His oxygen system, like all others, was a small white triangular mask that fitted over the nose and mouth. "You turned on the bottle, and that was it." Suddenly he blacked out almost completely, with only the dim, fuzzy knowledge that he was fainting and falling — straight down. He was within moments of crashing when he came to and managed to right his plane for the landing. Vomit had filled the oxygen tube to his mask. If he had not been a magnificent pilot, with well over two thousand hours in the air, he never would have been able to pull out. He would have gone straight in as Dick Haring did.

Malaria was like a complete poison vitiating every faculty, every organ, but in spite of it the pilots were continually in the air when they should have been stretched out in sick bays; and this was true of Beanie Payne, a man so utterly gentle and quiet that no one would suspect him of heroism either on the ground or in the air. Malaria would sometimes raise his temperature to 104 degrees. Yet under such conditions he like the others continued to fly, as soon as the shaking stopped.

# Fireworks over Guadalcanal

*nineteen*

★ The next day was October 23, the date of the biggest air battle that took place over Guadalcanal.[1]

"It was all dogfight," said Stout. "The Japs were throwing in everything to smash through to Henderson Field at last. Once they had made the field too bad a surface to use for takeoffs and landings, they could pour in troops and sweep the island clean. We kept in formation when we could, but mostly we had to go it alone. Most of the time nobody was guarding your tail. Zeros and Grummans were zooming, firing, coming from below, above, and both sides. Planes were spinning, looping, burning, slipping. The moisture in the air was just right for contrails, and the whole battle was written in loops through the air as though the sky were crazy. Bauer was so pleased and excited, when he talked about it, that he could hardly speak. He could only say, over and over, 'Godalmighty, that was a great fight; Godalmighty, that was a great fight!' Of course, it nearly killed him not to be up there, but he was the brain that guided the fight from the ground. If we could have had one Coach on the ground

198

to plan for us and one in the air to lead us, what wouldn't we have done? Crowds of planes were coming down in flames. Nobody in 212 forgot what Bauer had told us not long before: to stay with them and fight, no matter what the odds were, no matter how bad the position might be. That day we showed him we'd heard what he said.

"I managed to loop with a Zero that day. Usually they were so much more maneuverable than the heavy Grummans that we couldn't keep inside of them when they turned. Maybe he was a poor flyer, but I did a loop with him and got a burst solidly into him, and he went down in flames. Foss got one right at the top of his loop.

"That's when it's really flying, when you look down and see the sky full of writing, and a Grumman on the tail of a Zero and a Zero after that Grumman, and tracers flying past your head. I was after another Zero, and two Grummans headed in at the same target, and then right in front of us another Zero rose up, going so fast it looked as though he were diving up instead of down. All three of us opened up on him, and he just disintegrated. There wasn't a piece of him that ever hit the water. He just blew away in dust. I matched — that is, flipped a coin — with the other boys later on and lost, and so they got my third of that plane, because the authorities weren't crediting planes by thirds, only by halves.

And Stout continued: "I was having millions of misses as well as some hits up there, but now

I was nearly out of ammunition and had to leave. As I pulled away I saw five chutes coming down, and I considered strafing them with the few rounds I had left. I couldn't do it, but it was hard to let them get away when they might land in their own territory.

"That day two of our boys had to bail out, but we didn't lose a pilot. Afterwards the remark was, 'One of the Japs got away.' And someone else said, 'That's good. Let him go home and tell the story.' But another pilot said, 'No, he didn't make it. I got him at Savo.' That day was a real show for the Raiders in the front lines to watch, with the Zeros dropping like fireworks turned upside down. It was a morale builder, believe me."

Beanie Payne pulled a Zero down this day, and Baker of 212 got a double. Huckleberry Watkins also had a great day, with a brace of Japs shot down, but he can't remember any details. He recalls the biggest and most beautiful dogfight in the world, but what he did in it is vague to him. The Huckleberry type of hero lets the medals be pinned on other fellows, because he lacks enthusiasm for his own performances.

Rogers remembered that there was great teamwork between the Marine and Navy fighters, that October 23. Reese of Navy 72 was on Rogers's wing that day, and they were part of a big V that Major Leonard Davis of Marine Fighter Squadron 121 was leading toward the bombers, paying little attention to Zeros.

"But the Zeros were up there watching us the

way cats watch mice. As they got closer I turned into them head-on, because they had the altitude, but they didn't like to play the head-on game; perhaps it wasn't in their book of rules. The fellow that I went after gave me some evasive action, and I put in a burst when I could. Finally he did a roll — to confuse me, I suppose — but he made that roll just as I had him in my sights, and when he was over on his back I let him have it. He flickered off to the left and went down."

Freeman with another double swelled the 212 score, and Conger added to his growing total.

"It was like a hand of cards," said Conger, "a Zero, then a Grumman, another Zero, another Grumman, but I'd get too excited and keep missing. When I think of the stuff I had to shoot at, it makes me sick. You can't see how you missed. I centered one, though, and knocked a big puff of white smoke out of him. He started right home, losing altitude. I couldn't claim him, but I know he never got back.

"Then I found myself rising underneath and behind another Zero. He did a split S and came down a little. I slipped over to go after him and lost sight of him momentarily. And that is the trouble: things change so fast in the sky. You have your man, you miss him, you lose him — and maybe you've lost the whole world and yourself along with it. It happens while you're snapping your fingers a couple of times or making one pass.

"Then I saw my Zero again, pulling up and heading northwest. I poured wide-open throttle to it and went right after him. Somehow it was the biggest thrill I ever had. Now he was losing altitude, and I got above him, closing the gap a little more and a little more. In the meantime he'd been doing S turns, and I kept sliding over so that he wouldn't see me. Finally I got up to twenty or thirty yards — just like opening a door and walking into a room, it was so close. Then I fired the shortest burst I ever used, not more than twenty or thirty shots, but they were all smashing right home into him, and he blew up all over the sky — up there at twelve or thirteen thousand feet — and it was just like putting a stick of dynamite in this room. I was hoisted up in my seat by the force of the explosion."

And Conger added, "I saw the pilot blown up thirty feet in the air. The chute he had didn't open; and then he dropped, the chute flapping above him. Little pieces of the plane hung like leaves in the air. I came clear down and watched him hit the water. The shroud lines of the chute were holding him, and he was lying there as though asleep."

This day's fighting lifted the 212 score to sixty-five. It was this day that convinced Bauer that his team at last was right. Only a week ago they had landed in the dark hour, but in seven days they had given a good foretaste of what they could do.

October 24 followed a quiet night. Just before noon Bauer took off with Sigman, in response to a radar warning. It proved to be a false alarm, and Bauer came back safely, but 212 was deeply troubled. Up till now Bauer had confined himself almost entirely to the ground, which was the proper place for him as commander of the fighter strip, but the hunger for battle in the air was beginning to be too much for him. The October 24 flight gave 212 a prophetic shudder, for they knew there were wild horses in Bauer and hoped he would not be swept off his feet too often.

# One Day in the Life of Jack Conger

*twenty*

★ October 25 was Conger's wildest day. It had rained two whole days preceding, and everyone was in a foul humor, flooded out of tents, having to lie in brim-full slit trenches. On the morning of the twenty-fifth there was a mass of mud on the fighter strip. The colonel ordered the boys to check their planes thoroughly, but he would not try to scramble them in that mud unless there was a real emergency.

"Talk about real emergency!" said Conger. "Godalmighty, from eight in the morning to five in the afternoon there were Zeros over us all the time." When the first flight of them came over, Bauer told Foss of Squadron 121 to try to get a fighter off with flaps from the opposite end of the field where there still was some grass, and try to be airborne before he got to the muddy end of the field. Foss managed it, and then his whole flight followed him.

"Every twenty or thirty minutes the colonel would send up another flight, and as they got up to about fifteen thousand feet the Zeros would drop on them out of the sun. It used to seem certain that our flyers would be beaten right out of the air by those advantages of position and numbers, but Bauer's tactics of heading into the Zeros continued to win for us. Our men kept on shouldering Japs aside, so to speak. This was the day Chamberlain was wounded in the shoulder but managed to land his plane safely.

"The Japs came over in continuous waves, hard telling where from. We thought some must be carrier-based and some land-based. And as one wave tired itself out or went short on fuel, another wave would be coming in fresh. It was a tough day," said Conger. "About nine the colonel told Stout to scramble his outfit, which was Huckleberry, Drury, Freeman, Faulkner, and myself, but Freeman got stuck in the mud, and Huck's engine was so bad that he had to turn back to the field.

"As we climbed we saw three Jap cans [destroyers], and we could hear Cowboy calling over the radio, 'Control from Stout. . . . Do you want us to take the cans or the Zeros?' "

Stout continued the story: "As soon as I cleared the coconuts, I saw the beach and, wham! right in front of me were three Jap destroyers shelling our gun emplacements. Some of our little patrol boats — Mary Annes, they call them — had gone out and tied into the Japs, regardless of the differences in size and armament, and a couple of these boats were burning.

"I'd been smiling about the colonel, the way he'd been having fits that morning because it was so hard to get the planes off out of the mud. He was in fits, seeing us tied to the ground. 'What fun you boys would have if you could only get up there!' he kept saying, and he was so keen about it that he made us all grin at him. Well, we wiped the grins out when we saw the little patrol boats standing up to those destroyers, doing their duty and being smacked for it. That was when I hit the radio and called Operations to ask what I should do. Operations came back with 'Wait!'

"It's the damnedest thing how Operations is always answering, 'Wait!' Of course, Operations gets a broader, clearer picture of what's going on all over the sky, but when a flyer sees what he wants to do, it's hard to hear that 'Wait!' come over the air. You'll get it even when you're coming in for an emergency landing — because of course sometimes it's inadvisable to come right in, depending on how the Japs are hanging on their props, in what part of the sky.

"We kept circling, climbing, and at last got orders to strafe the cans. It sounded good to me, but before we were up another thousand feet orders came to go after the Zeros. And the next thousand there would be an order to strafe the cans. It went on like that until at twelve thousand feet the order was again to strafe the destroyers, so I didn't wait for them to change their minds again in Operations," Stout continued. "I dived on the middle can, a power dive with Conger after me, and the other two in our flight took the rear destroyer. Coming down close, I opened fire and just held right on to the burst, and I don't think a bullet missed the deck of that can. All three cans had opened up with anti-aircraft fire, but the boys came down a little too fast for the gunners to keep their aim. I pulled out too low and nearly hit the masthead. Conger just scraped over it, too."

"We really strafed them," said Conger of this exploit, which was to have such incredible results. "The cans were in column with black smoke pouring out of their stacks, making at least thirty knots, plus."

To Faulkner, attacking the last destroyer, "it looked as though the tracers were bouncing off the deck, but the armor-piercing bullets must have cut pretty deep into it. The men on the deck were not many in number, and believe me, they were giving us some evasive action; they scampered in every direction as fast as they could go. It was a fine, bright day, and I remember how white the bow waves were and how the wakes shone behind the destroyers."

It is well to get all the testimony of this strange event, and here is big Drury: "I concentrated on the center of that destroyer and put about twelve hundred rounds into it right there. I kept pushing the stick forward to hold my sights on the exact spot; so they gave us credit for half a destroyer apiece! When I pulled out I was right down on the water, going like hell."

The Australian coast-watcher on Santa Isabel Island reported, shortly after, that of the three destroyers, only one remained afloat. The other two had vanished. The concentrated strafing had apparently penetrated to the vitals of the lightly armored Jap cans. It has reportedly been demonstrated by our Navy that .50-caliber bullets getting into the turbines of a destroyer can shake it to pieces before the turbines can be shut down. However that may be, the two Japanese destroyers apparently vanished; and since the Navy did not attack any such targets on this day, the conclusion was that the plunging fire of the Grummans had caused their sinking — or so it was finally agreed by the authorities, who never gave credit unless there was good evidence for doing so. To the right side of 212's account, therefore, went two Jap destroyers, a feat not so far matched by fighter planes and mere machine-gun fire. When Bauer told his boys about the official crediting, it lifted them sky-high with confidence they could do just about anything.[1]

As he finished strafing, with every bullet spent, Stout spoke on the air to his wing man, Conger, and told him that his guns were empty, so Conger flew on Stout's wing back to the field, then turned off into the Zeros. Freeman joined up as they climbed for precious altitude.

In the meantime, Cloudy Faulkner had finished the strafing with a little ammunition left and on his way home ran into a Zero right over Henderson Field. He pulled a high-side on the Jap and sent him smoking, then came up from below and gave him a burst that knocked his left wing off.

The wing came down end over end, and the plane crashed in flames. "I don't think he ever saw me. He bailed out, and I believe he was the fellow that Conger afterwards pulled out of the sea. I circled the Jap as he was floating down, but I didn't shoot him. That sort of thing may be war, but it makes you sick.

"I tried to land, now that I had no bullets left, but a Zero was riding my tail. I made about three passes at the field, and each time I had to scoot away from the Zero again. Finally the anti-aircraft boys blasted him off and landed him in smoke. The AA fellows never got enough credit. They sat around getting cramps in their necks as they stared at the sky and prayed that one of our pilots would lure a Zero into their range. They were good, too. On one occasion three Zeros came over strafing the fighter strip, and the AA got them all in order, one, two, three."

Before Faulkner ran out of ammunition and had to land, Conger joined up on him above the field.

Conger continued: "I heard Control say that two Zeros were strafing the field, and sure enough, we saw two Zeros coming over the fighter strip. It was the first time in my life that I was above a Zero, I think, and it excited me so much that I dived down on him without the least conception of the speed the Grumman was developing. The result was that I ran right over him. I closed up so fast that I only had time to get in one short burst, and then I was flying past him.

Then I chased into the two Zeros over the beach, and we had a little dogfight there. I got in what felt like a good burst on one of them, but I couldn't observe the results because I had to get away from him with a flipper turn and headed at the other Zero. But the boys on the ground saw the first Zero smoke and go in, so he was given to me, though I didn't even claim him.

"The second fellow held his fire, and I held mine. We turned loose when we were close in, but I'd used up my last ammunition. It was time for me to get out of there, but somehow I hated to go. Maybe I was too excited. Maybe socking all those bullets into the Jap cans had made me feel as though these fellows were easy to take. Anyway, instead of clearing out I crouched down in my cockpit with the Zero firing at me and tried to think of something to do.

"It was a crazy thing to do. I can see that now, but at the time your brain doesn't add up one and one and make two; sometimes it makes a million.

"He'd got himself into a good position and came head-on in over me, very close. And I said to myself that if I eased back on the stick and came up just right, I'd be able to nick off his rudder with my propeller and bring him down. It sounds like suicide, but I wasn't thinking of anything like that. I was going to be very careful and foxy and just give his rudder a touch, you know?

"But when the moment came, instead of being

easy with the stick I came right back on it, and the first thing I knew — Jesus, crash!

"I'm not any too clear on just what happened, but the boys on the ground saw me hit him five feet from the rudder and slice him in two. Of course, the pilot didn't have a chance and went right straight in.

"What I knew was that I knocked my head against the gunsight, because for about three weeks afterwards I went around with a big lump on my jaw. I thought it would never go down.

"The collision had left me dizzy and stalled my plane, and it went into a spin about fifteen hundred feet up. That's a very short distance, if you want to do anything with a plane that's dropping in a spin. I tried to pull it out but couldn't. Maybe the prop was smashed, but I wasn't seeing or thinking very clearly. It was a right spin. The thing is to give opposite rudder, push forward on the stick, and then ease back; but the plane wouldn't come out.

"All at once I saw I was only a snap of my fingers away from going smash. I had to get away from that plane, and fast. I was so scared that just remembering it still takes the breath out of me. I had to tear away my oxygen mask and my earphones, and they seemed to stick. I pulled the hood back, unfastened the safety belt, and stood up. And there the weight of the slipstream hit me and glued me in place with a force like a cataract of water.

"I could only stand there, and my God, the sea

was jumping right up into my face. I managed to get my foot over the side of the cockpit at last, but my gun in a hip holster caught against the side of the cockpit, and my goggles went off in the wind, whew! (I hope you remember that we were only fifteen hundred feet up when that spin began!) And all these things were happening, and every second was split in about ten big chunks, each of them plenty big enough to die in.

"Now I was standing with one foot out and one foot in. I was pressed flat by the blast of the wind and held right there. And mind you, the way that sea was shooting up at me was a scary thing, and I could see the waves getting bigger and the shadows blacker. I was so scared that the fear must have given me a shot of adrenaline or something, because all at once I was able to move. I busted loose and made my jump.

"There wasn't time to count to ten. There wasn't time to count to two, even, before I pulled the rip cord. I was so close to the water that I still don't half believe that I'm alive. The boys from the strip saw the plane drop behind the coconut palms, and from that it was easy to figure out that I couldn't have been more than 250 feet above the sea. Dropping full speed from that height, the sea is supposed to smash you flat, as though it were a pavement. I just grabbed that rip cord and yanked. If I'd missed the first grab there never would have been time to make another. But I was lucky. Oh, man, was I lucky! That old parachute didn't wait to be asked twice but just blossomed right out and slowed me up with a terrific jerk.

"I just had time to swing on the shroud lines this way, that way, twice; then I went crash in the water. That was too close. That was a lot too close.

"I must have hit the water awfully hard. That day, with all the excitement, I wasn't sore at all. But the next morning I felt as though I'd had the hell beat out of me. You know when you've had a bad fall you feel it in the small of your back; well, the small of my back the next day was too sore to touch."

Conger continued: "Going back to that moment, I was pretty far under water and not thinking clearly, not thinking at all, I guess. Why I didn't fight my way straight up to the surface, and get tangled in the shroud lines, and drown there under the parachute, I don't know. Maybe some instinct was working for me in the place of good sense, but anyway I swam out to the side and came clear of the lines.

"I got clear of my chute straps, and then I popped my life jacket; I mean that I touched off the cartridges that generated the gas to inflate my life jacket. It's a funny thing that hardly a morning had passed that I didn't begin the day by opening the slots of those cartridges and making sure that the charges were good. And just as I reached for those cartridges, it came over me like a fall of a house that this was the only morning I'd failed to do it. And this would be the last time I'd need life jackets or anything else, if they failed me now. That was a tough half-second. I think it scared me almost as much as being up there in the spinning plane. Well, this must sound just like a fake, because I was scared to death only while I was reaching for those cartridges; when I popped them, they worked fine. But let me tell you, while the scare was on my mind I promised myself that if I ever lived through this, I'd be a mighty careful boy and go through all the right motions. My *Lord!*

"I never did see my plane, but I suppose it hit the water and went right on down. I was about to start swimming when I looked up, and there in the sky I saw a Zero that some Grumman [Faulkner's] had given a dose of .50s to. It went screwing up into the air burning like the devil, and then it came down and exploded as it hit the sea not a hundred feet from me. And it kind of seemed to me that a lot of things were happening in my neighborhood that day.

"The next I saw was the Jap pilot of that plane. He had bailed out, and now he was floating down as easy as you please. He wore a dark suit, and as he landed in the water not twenty yards from me I could see by his ugly mug that he was a Jap, all right. A good old Higgins boat had spotted me and was coming out to fetch me in, so I just lay there and floated. First they stopped by the Jap, but he waved them away, so they came out to me and left him there to rot. I told the Marines in the boat that we'd go back now and stop where the Jap was. 'Sure,' they said, 'we'll stop there long enough to shoot him.' There's no two ways about it, the boys just simply don't like the Japs very well. But I pointed out to them that we hadn't taken a Jap aviator prisoner as yet, and that we might get some worthwhile information out of him. They grumbled a bit at this but went over and stopped beside him, and I motioned him to climb on board.

"He simply kicked himself away from the boat. Well, it made me feel a little queer. I suppose it's all right for a fellow to be willing to fight until he dies, but war shouldn't be just plain murder. In a way it ought to be just a game that you play extra hard. And as I looked down at the Jap there in the water, I didn't admire him. I didn't respect him at all. I simply felt that there was a lot of the ornery devil in him. There was, too, as you're going to see.

"I took a grappling hook and reached over the side of the boat and got the hook fastened right under the shoulder of his life jacket. I started lifting up on it with a sailor helping me, and we hoisted the Jap waist-high out of the sea. And then the son of a bitch pulled a gun out of his belt! I didn't see it, but a Marine yelled to me to look out, and the next thing I knew, that bastard had the gun right in my face and pulled the trigger. There was just a click; the cartridge was wet and didn't explode. Me? I did a sort of backflip to get away and landed on the other side of the Higgins boat.

"They say he tried to shoot himself next, but still the gun wouldn't work. I scrambled back to the rail where several Marines were taking aim, and believe me, they looked as though they were enjoying themselves, too. But I yelled and made them put their guns down. I looked at the Jap, and somehow I was really burned. I took one of those five-gallon jerry cans, and I reached over and slugged him over the head with it. I wanted to stun him, but if I had bashed in his brains it wouldn't have broken my heart completely. However, a Jap's skull is made of India rubber. The blow just knocked him about twenty feet down under water, and when he drifted up again he was still wearing that mean look and wouldn't get in the boat.

"I picked up a boat hook and whacked him over the head and opened a gash half a foot long in his scalp, and a sailor whanged him with a grappling hook. All this before his lights went out and we could drag him on board the boat.

"There he was, looking wet and soggy and small, and we gave him first aid and admired the way he was dressed. His togs were damned smart. He wore a heavy gabardine flying suit, dark brown, and over this was a tight-fitting kapok life jacket. He had on leather flying boots and a leather helmet when I first saw him land, but he'd taken these off and they were lost. Under the flying suit he had a warm cloth jacket, but to keep his damned neck warm he had on the top of a turtleneck sweater and a scarf about five yards long of the finest silk. His pistol was a very neat Mauser automatic. He had his airplane clock tied around his neck, and he had a map of the Solomon Islands and New Guinea. He had courses on it marked from Bougainville and Guadalcanal on down to Buna and Port Moresby, et cetera. We took it from this that he'd been on a number of missions before this last one. So after we'd picked him like gifts from a Christmas tree, we turned him over to Intelligence to see what they could get out of him. I got the scarf and shirt as souvenirs. What I really wanted was that fine pistol, but good things like that just evaporate when there are handy American Marines and sailors around. You take a first-rate Marine, and if he wants a thing, really, it stands up on legs and walks to him.

"A doctor came," Conger went on, "and plastered up that Jap's head with ointments and bandages, while a jeep carried me over to the field. The boys seemed pretty glad to see me, but not half as glad as I was to see them. The colonel wanted to know every detail of what I'd had in mind when I rammed the Jap. I tried to make it sound like a sensible plan, but after a while he began to laugh, and then I had to laugh, too. He said that anything I could get away with was all right. Then he frowned and told me not to get so excited the next time. But he was happy enough. When his boys were knocking Zeros out of the sky and coming back alive, he was the happiest man on earth, and we all knew it. If you did anything that was halfway good, he made it seem just twice as fine.

"I couldn't fly the next day or the next, I was so stiff and sore from that whack on the hard face of the sea. That gave me a chance to go up and see my Jap in the prison camp. I thought after he'd calmed down he might even be a little grateful to me — which only showed that I didn't understand the Japs. He just stared at me, very mean, his eyes never shifting, as though he were picking out the place where he'd like to put a knife into me.

"He said that he was a graduate of Tokyo University. He had been flying about two years, and he was twenty, now. He answered the questions slowly, and you could see that he didn't want to talk to us. But maybe his face was hurting him — it was all bandaged.

"He had been flying in a lot of action, in China, Java, and the Battle of the Coral Sea. In that fight he'd shot down an American plane. I remember how he grinned when he said this. He'd been flying out of Bougainville, just lately. That's about all I can recall about him. He was burned around his eyes from the flames in his cockpit before he could bail out. He spoke pretty good English, and I think he was a Jap of the highest class — samurai, or whatever it is."[2]

So ends Jack Conger's description of a day that I think could rank with almost any that we can pick out of the lives of the most venturesome

American heroes. There was no vanity in a single word, and as he talked to me there was not the slightest bid for applause. As for the action, it was all the sharpest excitement, and I believe he was happiest in recalling the pleasure of the colonel.

# The Coach's Boys Raid Rekata Bay

*twenty-one*

★ There were a couple of quiet days after that, distinguished by the return of King, a big ebullient Irishman from Boston. Having been shot down, King hit shallow water not far from the coast of Santa Isabel Island some seventy miles north of Guadalcanal, and the natives dragged his plane ashore. He destroyed its radio equipment and let his rescuers have a good time with the rest of the ruined plane. "I showed them how to take the cowling off, and they danced around with the bright stuff held over their heads, as happy as children." It was during this time that King secured information about Rekata Bay at the northern part of the island that led to devastating raids on that Jap stronghold, for here Tojo was fond of starting reconnaissance flights over Guadalcanal and other places, and here he was pooling ammunition and oil dumps and collecting planes for his raids. To the colonel it looked like a fat prize, and he decided to send the "Stout Boys," as Cowboy's flight was sometimes called, to feel out the position and do what damage they could.

It was a long flight and a dangerous one, because no one could tell how many interceptors the Japs could put in the air. The hope was to catch the enemy napping with his float-planes on the water. Intelligence agreed that the job ought to be taken in hand, and now that 212 had built its score up to over seventy, it was expected to take on the tough jobs in all directions. The maps brought in by King would give the boys extra precision in reading the face of the jungle and hunting for installations.

On October 28, at about eight in the morning, Stout took off with Drury, Faulkner, Watkins, Conger, Rogers, and Freeman; and there were three Army pilots along flying the P-39s which had not distinguished themselves in air combat but were useful for strafing and bombing in close support of the front lines around Guadalcanal. About 9:15 they came over the shallows of Rekata Bay, scooped into the coastline with the forest green pouring almost down to the shore. Even with the charts provided by King it was a fairly blind business. The colonel had given some unusual instructions: planes shot up on ground or water were to be attributed to the whole squadron, not to individual members. His aim was thus to inculcate team spirit. It might be just slightly more efficient to shoot planes afloat on the bay, but he hoped to have the ducks rise before they were bagged. He said, "Scare them up. Let 'em think they're going to have a fighting chance, and then give 'em hell."

Rogers recalled, "Rekata was a nice-looking place, with a peninsula sticking out there and the bay in here, wide-mouthed to some of the winds. As we came over we could see seven float-Zeros and some scout biplanes, wavering with the motion of the water a little, and right under the surface there were two big bombers somebody had damaged so that they barely lasted to the bay and then sank. We made a circle to wake up the pilots of the Zeros, then went down and strafed them as some of them began to rise.

"We got nearly all of those Zeros, and then we had to pay attention to the shore installations. That's where King's map came in so well, because he'd marked down every machine-gun nest. Still, they were putting up a lot of ack-ack, and those gunners were good, too. We silenced some of them by killing off the gun crews, but there was always a good deal of fire from the guns. As the fight mixed up and we lost the positions of some of the machine guns, we'd dive blind at the jungle, and then when a nest of ack-ack opened up we'd have a target to shoot at. They had plenty of 20-mm stuff too, and they knew how to use it.

"We caught glimpses of Tojo's boys running around in the jungle, and the faces of some of them looked like wide-open screaming as we dove low." And here again our boys noted that the Jap, when he is all set and established, with something laid out for him to do and all his thinking done for him, is a patient and courageous fighter who carries on until he dies; but if he is taken by surprise, his wits are apt to be scrambled, and he runs around rather like a squirrel in a cage. The first Rekata job was finished off by setting two gasoline dumps on fire, and Stout led his flight away with huge black plumes of mourning feathering the air above Rekata Bay.

On the way back to Guadalcanal one of the Army pilots, with the distinctive name of Jones, lost all of the coolant from his engine and bailed out over the jungle. "The natives took good care of him. That was before they learned that the Tojo boys were poison and the Americans were not. They had a Jap with them, and they were treating him fine, but this Jones was a brainy guy, and after he'd been around for a while he made it clear to the natives that he wasn't very happy. They wanted to know why, and he told them it was pretty hard on him to be there with empty hands while the Jap was sporting a fine automatic pistol. What made it so hard, he said, was because the Jap had swiped the pistol from him! Well, the natives figured on this for a while, and they couldn't stand thinking about that kind of a thief, so they got the pistol for our side, and then Jones took the Jap prisoner and brought him all the way in."

About this time our High Command decided to expand our perimeter around Henderson Field and give our ground forces more elbow room. Reinforcements were coming in from Tulagi by night, and there were conferences at headquarters to work out the best schemes for using fighter planes in the planned offensive. It was Bauer's idea that another stroke at Rekata Bay might be effective, and it was decided to try a second raid, but this time at the crack of dawn in case Tojo should be on the alert for another daytime attack.

Stout said, "Somebody figured out the timing just wrong, because to get there just at dawn would be fine, but to get there in the dark would be playing blindman's bluff, and that's no good in the air. I argued that we were scheduled to start too early, but what weight does a second lieutenant carry when it comes to giving advice?

"It was black as a coat closet at 5:15 that morning when we took off, and the weather was as bad as the Japs could have wished it. We had to go by our instruments, flying around rainstorms with the wind going crazy now and then, but we kept the navigation correct and came in on the coast not far from our target. I knew by that time what I had only guessed before, that we were going to reach Rekata Bay a long, long time before the sunrise, and it made me feel rotten. Even by daylight it can be hard enough for the boys in a flight to take care of one another and keep the Zeros off the other fellow's tail, but darkness makes everything a crazy gamble. And whatever happens to a flight is the leader's fault, and that's the way it should be.

"As we came in toward the bay I told the flight to turn off all running lights. As a matter of fact,

I had a hard time turning off my own, but by the flashing of the exhausts I counted my planes and saw that the formation was intact. Now we were over the bay, and there were two lights on it where seaplanes were warming up for a dawn takeoff. I told the boys to go after them, and I took the first one. Of course, I had a hope, as my plane bore down through the darkness, that that Jap would be on his toes enough to get himself into the air before I hit him. But I didn't have any luck; he was still squatted on the water when my tracers began to smash into him. He began to burn — it's remarkable how long a plane will burn on the water — and it was like a candle held up in a dark room, lighting the Zeros on the bay for us.

"By the time I'd passed over and pulled up in a wingover, the second of the first pair of Zeros was burning also, and all at once I began to have hope that, darkness or not, this might be another good day for the Coach. The AA was opening up now, the tracers streaking up from the ground and turning over at the end in a rainbow curve. I began to strafe the emplacements, and when I spotted a stream of tracers, I'd dive and give the source of the fire a burst. I looked back across the water, and there was light enough from the burning planes to show the wakes of the other Zeros as they got in motion, so I called the flight and told it that the Japs were taking off. I went on doing wingovers and strafing the guns.

"I was pulling into one of those wingovers when I saw a Zero against the light in the east. There wasn't much shining over there, but you know before the day begins how a pale streak comes in the east and stays there a long time — nothing to see by, but strong enough to make a silhouette? This Zero surprised me, and I had to bank around sharply, trying to get on his tail. Then I saw that he had his running lights on, the fool, and his 20-mm was belching at another plane right ahead of him — one of my boys, I thought sure, and with running lights on, too. I grabbed the mike and yelled, 'Turn off your lights! Turn off your lights!' But while I was yelling, he burst into flames and hit the water.

"One of us was gone. There didn't seem to be any doubt of that, and it was a hard sock for me, because I never had lost one of my boys before. And all at once I sure wanted to get the Zero that had done that job. He pulled up at a pretty sharp angle, against the east, and then I had him bore-sighted and I gave it to him. My tracers slammed into him. I could see them dancing in his cockpit, and then it was a whirl of flames. He lighted up like a Christmas tree, then he went down and in.

"That made it one for one, but that wasn't enough. Twenty Japs for one of 212 wouldn't have been half enough, the way I was feeling just then. We only had enough gas for about fifteen minutes of fighting, besides the return flight, so I called the boys and told them to start home."

Stout's narrative is only one of the many angles on that memorable battle in the black of night with the pale streak of dawn just beginning to lighten the east. The fighting largely took place under fifteen hundred feet, and that, of course, is difficult because there's no room to maneuver. Drury says — unemotional as he is — that he would rather hit dirt than the face of the sea when going at speed, "because you can plough a furrow in the dirt, but when you slap the sea it's like running into a concrete wall."

His impression of that night fight over Rekata Bay was of tracers coming out of nowhere, and planes appearing and disappearing. It was like fifteen minutes spent in a cave full of bats, except these bats could kill you with a touch. "We had our lights out, of course, and when a Jap saw a shadow of a plane coming, he'd blink his lights. When we didn't answer, he'd leave his on — so as to keep from being hit by a pal, I suppose, but it was a mighty foolish business because it gave us their lights to shoot at, and you can't ask for anything much better than that where there's a brawl in the air at night. I remember going after one Zero who was zigzagging all over the sky in evasive action, and when I was just about to open up on him, another plane — one of our boys, as it turned out later — came in from my left and started firing tracers that seemed to flick right across my nose. I blinked; the second fellow was gone, and I was still on the tail of my man. I ended up with only one gun, firing at his little white taillight, and it seemed to be right in my sights. Then he dipped over and went straight in. It was a big enough splash to see even in the night.

But when I got back to the field I found three .50-caliber bullet holes in the star on my left wing, put there by whoever it was who'd come to help me work on my Zero at such close range!"

Watkins also brought down a Zero with only one of his guns firing. "I saw a sea-biplane such as they used for scouting coming out of the west, going home, I suppose. I went after him, and the rear-seat gunner put some shots right behind my head. I followed him right around until I lost him against the black of the sky, but Freeman was behind me and saw him head down into the jungle and crash."

Nothing the pilots put into words reproduces their sense of the black smother of night with the brief arcs of ack-ack flashing in the sky. They try to describe it, but they are left reaching for words. Conger said, "You couldn't be sure of anything except by flying into the west and then turning back. Against the misty light in the east I could see float-planes, and I knew those were Japs and went after them. Flying that way, if anything came at me I was sure that he couldn't see me in his path. One did come, and I turned on his tail into a perfect position, but when I got there I could barely make him out; a black silhouette against black isn't easy to see. We were getting down lower and lower when I opened up on him, and he snapped around and flew right at me. He was almost flying down my throat before I got him lined up and gave him a good burst. He did a split S right into the water."

It was Conger's tenth and last plane, and it made a double ace of him. Earlier in the fight he had zoomed down on a Zero and blown the bits of it all over the bay. Freeman, for his part, had destroyed a parked biplane and made five strafing runs after doing his work on the Zeros but received no enemy fire from the ground.

The hardest part of the raid for its commander was the misery of the return to Henderson Field with the certainty that one of his men had "gone in."

Stout made his report to Bauer hardly caring what impression his words made, for his eye was on the clock, which, as the seconds went by, was proving more and more clearly that the missing plane was indeed lost. Bauer himself listened to the report in silence, also eyeing the clock. Seven planes were in, and the eighth still lagged hopelessly behind. Beyond all this, the plane Stout had seen a Zero shoot down must have been an American casualty, it seemed, unless in the confusion of the battle the Zero had turned his guns on a friend.

But then the far-off roar of a plane came like music to the watchers. Out of place and out of time — impossibly late, in fact — plane number eight, Drury, did actually drop down onto the fighter strip and made the Rekata Bay night mission a complete success.

# Cloudy Faulkner's Plane Retrieved from Espiritu Santo

*twenty-two*

★ It was about this time that Bauer began to worry about the plane in which Cloudy Faulkner had made an emergency landing on the beach of Espiritu Santo. He knew the propeller was ruined. But if that were replaced, it was hoped that the ship might navigate again, and Grummans were more valuable than aviators on Guadalcanal at this time. So Bauer sent Stout in a Higgins boat to see what could be done. The plane was said to be standing on its nose, but there was enough hope to make the trip worthwhile.

Stout said, "There were three Navy men who ran the boat, and we had some mechanics along from 212 to do the repairing and replace the prop and all that. It was hotter than hell, but we made a good trip and in the middle of the night ran the Higgins boat up on an open beach.

"We could see a native village off there, and we made a quiet camp because we didn't know whether the black boys would be friendly or hostile. We ate emergency rations that night, but they're not very satisfying, and the next morning we sent two or three men to the village ahead of the rest of us, because if the natives are scary, sometimes they'll be alarmed by numbers. But there wasn't a soul to be found, anywhere. It was a huge village, and it looked lived in but not recently.

"We prepared to go back to sea and were about to push off when we heard a rustling in the grass, and three natives appeared, all badly frightened. One of them was dying and deformed by elephantiasis." They spoke a little English, but it was very hard for Stout and the others to understand what was said. Vaguely, like objects seen in a heavy fog, these facts emerged. The villagers had been getting along very well when there was a raid of "Big Men" from the hills, who carried away all the women. That would have been enough to finish off the village eventually, but elephantiasis took hold of the survivors and finished off the job rapidly. Only these three remained. That was the story as the men of 212 understood it.

"The headman didn't know where Faulkner's plane was, but he offered to show us where the next tribe was, so we took him on board, and that afternoon we spotted the wreck of Cloudy's ship on the beach and landed. The plane looked pretty much done in, standing on its nose that way, but we knew that our mechanics could bring even a skeleton of a Grumman to life. So we began by lassoing the tail wheel and dragging the wreck back to the ground.

"Pretty soon the chief of the local tribe ventured out to talk to us. He had more English words than the others, and a few American cigarettes warmed him up and gave him confidence. He called the plane the Big Pigeon. He had talked to Faulkner and called him Cloudy. He signaled and brought in more of the tribe. It was queer to watch them coming, a step at a time, ready to bolt and beginning to smile by degrees. But pretty soon they saw that we didn't bite, and then all at a stroke they became confident and easy. Except for Faulkner, it was a long time since they had seen white men, and their tribal legends must have painted the whites in good light. They were really friendly. They were so damned friendly that it made us feel human nature is naturally pretty decent and kind until the hard-handed guys show up and begin to throw their weight around. You couldn't help thinking about the difference — I mean, between these fellows and the Japs. They were just as opposite to us in ways and appearance as the Japs; they were more so. But they hadn't yet been taught how to hate strangers.

"It made us feel queer, as though the war were clear around on the other side of the world and had nothing to do with us. You might say it was like being farther away from the war than home would be, even. Those natives were so bighearted that it made us a little sad. Right away they began bringing us gifts. They came in a long procession, and since I was the headman of our outfit, they put down the stuff at my feet. It made a whale of a heap in no time. A chap would come along staggering under the weight of a basket of fruit that was about all he could handle, and I'd pay him off with one cigarette. He'd go and sit down on his heels and smoke that cigarette, perfectly happy. He seemed happier with the cigarette than I was with the fruit. And I didn't know how to pay him better than that. When we ran out of cigarettes, we gave them odds and ends and trinkets.

"It was funny, but not funny enough to make you laugh. When they'd made their gifts, each of them went off and squatted, not facing our big fire or one another, but turning in any direction, like animals in a corral.

"I told the chief that I wanted to give him something. He seemed to think that cigarettes were enough, and he couldn't think of anything else to ask for. I tried a compass on him, and though I don't think he understood just what it was good for, he could make out that the needle kept pointing in one direction, and of course that was magic. It bowled him over. I gave him a flashlight too, and that was something extra-special: cold fire that would show you your way through the jungle at night!

"Sigman was along. We used to call him Souvenir Sig, he was so keen on picking up stuff, and naturally he knew just exactly what would please another fellow. He brought out a mirror and demonstrated it to the chief. The flash of the mirror set the chief up on his toes, watching like a cat and ready to jump. Finally he noticed his own face in the glass. I suppose he didn't recognize himself, but Sig kept saying, 'You know him? Him fellow you!' And finally he caught on. He poked his finger against his nose, and the image in the glass did the same thing. That nearly capsized the headman with excitement. He got up and ran for his village to show the miracle all around to the rest of his people.

"The next day the natives seemed to feel that they'd had all the best of the bargain, and they kept on bringing down truck till there was more than we could take away in the Higgins boat.

"What we wanted most was water, and it was hard to make them understand that. I did everything I could, and they kept shaking their heads while our tongues parched. Finally I tried pouring a bit of the last water in my canteen on my hands, and they got the idea from that. However, they were very chary of their water; I had an idea that they used coconut milk in place of water most of the time."

Gunner Ross said, "No, they can't live on coconut juice. And on the little islands there aren't any streams or lakes, most of the time. But these fellows hollow out bowls in the hardest rocks, and there the rainwater collects. But there never is much of it, and so they go easy with the stuff."

Cowboy said, "The natives sat, at least a hundred of them, all night long, looking at us, or staring out to sea, or facing the jungle — just glad, apparently, to be there. We had guards posted, and the next morning all the tribesmen seemed to be in exactly the same posture. They hadn't moved a bit; maybe they sleep sitting up."

Gunner Ross said, "These bozos can sing, all right, and in parts that harmonize. Beautiful bass and mezzo-soprano voices, deep and rich. And when they have a big singsong, they sure beat hell out of the ground with their stomping."

"We tried to contact the women of the village," said Stout. "Sigman and I went in and wanted to take pictures. The chief seemed quite happy about it and had tom-toms beaten to collect all the men and the boys. Sig finally spied a woman and wanted to get her into the picture, but the chief wouldn't have it. He got very mad and made himself clear on the point. We gathered that these people are pretty liberal about most of their possessions, but they don't want to lose their pigs or their women."

Business, however, was a different matter. "If we wanted to buy a girl, that was all right. The chief had a daughter that he brought out and showed off to us. He rated her at eight pigs, but we thought that was a little high."

Sigman was the fellow who got along best with the natives. "I never saw anything like it. Whether they understood or not, he kept right on talking to them, and they loved it. He had them hypnotized. He took them down to the plane and put the earphones of the radio over their ears and explained the whole complication of radio theory and practice to them. Of course, they didn't understand a word of that rigmarole, but they were entirely happy, and so was Sig. I think he would have been glad to live and die there, he liked those good-natured people so much, and before he'd been there a year he would have taught them all about mechanical things; he had all the patience in the world. And inside that same year he would have been king of the island, you can bet. Or a whole flock of islands, for that matter."

Gunner Ross said, "All the natives are good people to begin with. It's the missionaries that ruin them with cracky ideas and buying and selling. All they understand is *giving,* at first. There's honesty and a code among them until along come the missionaries. Then they begin to steal and kill. The best missionaries are the Catholics. I'm an Irish damn Protestant, but the Catholic religion was the best goddamn religion we ever had for the natives. I can hand the biggest goddamn hand to it of all the goddamn religions."

Stout continued: "It took all the hand power we could get out of ourselves and the natives to move the plane from the soft to the hard sand where it might be possible to take off. We had done what we could about the engine. The oil was drained and changed, and the filters were changed, too. I had natives on both wings to rock back and forth and clear us a bit from the sand, and when everything was set we started the engine. The mechanics had flooded it a bit, and there was a burst of flame and big smoke that sent all the natives kiting for the woods. We had the beach all to ourselves for the takeoff. It wasn't too easy, because the strip of sand was so narrow that one wheel was practically in the sea. However, I got in the air, and the others came back by the Higgins boat. Afterwards we sent back stuff to the blacks, a lot of gadgets and cigarettes by the carton.

"That was a good trip. The war went to sleep ten years and ten thousand miles away; it was hard for me to believe that the plane could take me back to Henderson Field in such a short time."

# A Memorable Night on "the Canal"

*twenty-three*

★ November was the month that almost broke the Marine line on Guadalcanal and finally broke the heart of Tojo instead. This was when he made his all-out effort by air, land, and sea. And it was in the first days of November that Sergeant DeBenedictis of the 212 ground force escaped the peaceful boredom of life on Efate by hitching a ride to Guadalcanal. Those were days when it looked as though the Marines were to be expended in a holding operation that would cost the Japs much time and the life of every American on Guadalcanal; but DeBenedictis was blessed with the sort of curiosity that gets boys into trouble. He is a stalwart young fellow with the swarthy complexion of his Italian ancestors, the persuasive manners of his race, a husky, whispering voice, and an insatiably critical eye for men and events. So he talked his way onto a plane for Guadalcanal and gives us a description of what he found there.

He found the men under Bauer's direction on the fighter strip at Henderson Field bogged down in miserable living conditions, their minds too given to the labor of fighting, their bodies too exhausted by it, to have imagination to plan or strength to create even a slightly better environment. When he reported to his commander, the colonel was holding a conference in a tent a foot deep with water and slime, his conferees stretching their legs out on boxes to keep partly from the wet. DeBenedictis made some suggestions, and Bauer told him to carry them out. There were not many hands available to create the rude elements of a camp, but DeBenedictis took what he could find and rallied out some of the hospital cases who could hobble about. With this meager force he managed to create a bit of comfort for the men on the drained slope of "the hill," that low ridge which was the backbone of the American position.

Every day the work went on at the camp; every night the Japanese pressure increased, because of course it was at night that they attacked. The firing had a way of seeming to creep closer and closer until it seemed impossible to keep the boys of Tojo out, and one gap in the thin, bending line of the Marines would be enough to let the flood of murder in. In the morning DeBenedictis went out to see what kept the Marines intact.

He found them scattered in an irregular line of foxholes, slit trenches, and occasional strong points. All around them the jungle had been whittled away to stumps and shreds by bullets and shells. They were not all Raiders. The great majority were ordinary Marines with no special training, but all were volunteers, and all were bearded and dirtied, prematurely aged by unrelenting combat, their faces hollow-eyed from strain and fatigue and yellowed by malarial fever. Their thin line was a string of individuals, as a rule, yards apart from one another, each a vital link in a frail cordon.

Beyond their positions DeBenedictis glimpsed the barbed wire that tangled through the bullet-wrecked jungle. Dead Japanese were draped on it. A Jap tactic was to charge in successive waves and cover the barbs of the wire with the dead of the first wave, over which succeeding waves could charge on toward the Americans. The Marines disregarded those gruesome figures, rotting and stinking in the sun in front of them. "They had to, or they would have gone out of their minds." Instead, during this daytime lull in the fighting they busied themselves with the minutiae of their strange existence, minutiae that affirmed a kind of normalcy in the face of horrors almost too terrible to think about. Thus DeBenedictis found them, mainly engaged in trading souvenirs taken from the enemy, those Japanese who had crossed the apron of flesh hanging from the wire and met their death, sometimes hand to hand, as they closed with our boys.

Helmets, knives, guns, and a variety of personal belongings were involved in this macabre exchange, though helmets were cheap unless a pattern of bullet holes had been stitched into them. Mauser automatic pistols were highly prized. A pity, it was generally felt, that most of the silken underwear, such as lucky fellows found on Jap officers, was too small for Americans to wear. There were scarves decorated with figures of nude females. Jap flags were the most prized souvenirs of all, but there were not many of these, and they usually became unit rather than personal trophies. So the living and the dead were united in a strangely intimate way, as has been more or less true in this manner in all wars everywhere.

Our men, holding night after night against absurd odds, thinking that each darkness and each daylight may be their last, are not anxious to talk about warfare. They prefer to put their minds on other matters, but when queried by DeBenedictis they made light — perhaps by reason of necessity, for if a man fears his enemy too greatly, he may become paralyzed when the moment of action arrives — of anyone who believes that it is wise to screech like hysteria when making an attack.

"The Nips get doped up or drunk, and then they come, caterwauling. Those Imperial Marines are nearly as bad as the rest. They yell their heads off. You take one of our boys the other night, he let their screaming get under his skin, and he started damning the Japs for fools at the top of his lungs. He'd let off a blast of bullets and then damn some more and dare them to come on. He told them they'd never get through the wire. So the attack dies down a little, and then the morning comes and stops the shooting, and right out there in reaching distance of that mug's foxhole there's five Japs lying cut up with a machine-gun burst. They'd sneaked through the wire, all right — perhaps while he was damning them — and so there they lay because he'd hit them by accident and never knew they were near. The sight of them kind of silenced him. It made him sort of thoughtful."

It made DeBenedictis thoughtful, too. "It was lonely work," he said. "Goddamn lonely work. Imagine yourself out there all by yourself, knowing it all depends on you, not only your life but the lives of all your buddies." How effective was the lonely work of the Marines on that line at Guadalcanal is expressed by the eight or nine Japs who died for every American who gave up his life, and this in spite of enormous superiority in manpower and matériel.

There had to be an ultimate moment, a darkest hour, and it came before DeBenedictis had been long on the island.[1]

In the days preceding there had been signs of increased Jap activity; it was known that fresh artillery had been landed by them, together with new forces of infantry. On this night the very first crash of the guns after sunset told the Marines what was coming, and each man, lonely at his post, felt the added danger like wind in his face. "They just loosened up and poured it on us," said DeBenedictis. "They plastered the line, the hill, the jungle, every inch of our position, and I knew that we couldn't hold them off. I'd seen

242

how thin our troops were stretched, and through the holes the Japs were bound to leak. It would be like trying to hold water in a sieve."

It was the kind of time when it's easy to give up; the night was so black, and the wind seemed to puff the darkness in your face. "There was some light, but it came in cracks and snatches from the tracers whiplashing across the sky. That kind of light doesn't do you much good, because you know the other fellow is using it to see you by. You get a blink-blink-glimmer, and then crash comes a shell, or the ripping of machine-gun bullets. And all the while I kept remembering that the Marines had had all they could do several times before. They were tired, now, and they were sick. And now they were having it poured to them twice as heavy as ever before.

"The Nips began to plaster our hill, and pretty soon the hospital wasn't tenable. That meant we had to move the sick and wounded. We had some bad cases that were waiting evacuation, men so badly hurt that I thought they'd fall apart when we lifted them, and there were malaria cases with chills and fever shaking their bones. There were fellows groaning, but they didn't groan any more when we picked them up; and they wouldn't let their teeth chatter, because it might sound as though they were afraid. We got them all to the farther side of the hill, wrapped up in blankets or whatever we could find. Some of them were out of their heads, but now their minds cleared up fast because they knew what was coming. They knew that surrendering was out of the question. There are a lot of painful ways to die, heart trouble and poison and all that, but nothing compares with death-by-Jap, because they're experts and know by instinct all the nerve centers. It's not pleasant to have your eyes cut out or your balls cut off. I saw fellows so sick that a minute before, they hardly cared whether they lived or died; but they started caring right now and began to scratch the ground to make foxholes."

And DeBenedictis continued: "All the while the gunfire got heavier and heavier. The rifle bullets flicked by close to your ear, the machine-gun stuff rattled like bursts of heavy rain, and the shells came in with a rip and a wow looking for you. There's this about any steady fire: the source seems to keep coming closer and closer. You could feel the Japs pressing in, and then during patches of half-silence there were voices howling. When you hear a sound like that it gives you the willies. You think of a man already dying but enough alive to make a last run at you. You think of a face gone crazy with pain and coming at you like a nightmare. Then somebody said close to my ear, 'It's all over; they've got us!' I listened, and my brain wouldn't understand. The guy went on: 'They've broke through, behind the hill!' I told him to shut up, because I didn't want the hospital cases to hear. But a rumor like that can penetrate farther and faster than an armor-piercing shell, and before I could turn around the sick men had the word.

"If the Japs had broken through our line then, the invalids were cooked; we were all cooked.

"I got a glimpse of the trees along the base of the hill below us where they must have cut through, and the trees themselves seemed to be creeping closer. Well, we managed to get a rifle, a pistol, some sort of a weapon, to every one of the boys out there on the hill, and they damned the Japs a little and got ready to do their last shooting. If Tojo's boys thought the hospital would be a soft touch, they had a surprise coming. I began wondering, though, why, if the Japs had cut through, some of our men from the broken line hadn't fallen back to where we were. But then I realized what must have happened. Those Marines in the line would not be falling back. They'd know, all of them, that one breakthrough was death for the whole outfit; they'd die where they stood. So Tojo had won out, at last! But still he'd find when he got to us that there were hornets stinging till the last man was finished. There was a strange comfort in the feeling I'd had from the first that this was to be the last stand on Guadalcanal. From the very first the Marines had been put up there to be expended and save vital time for somebody, somewhere. And this was the finish."

DeBenedictis's voice grew quieter as he told what followed: "It seemed a little queer, however, that the Japs didn't pour right through and swallow us up, but I could understand that, too. Having cut open a gap, they were gathering reinforcements so as to pour in a bigger wave on us and put out all the lights in a single rush. Then something moved on the hill below. I got ready to shoot. I suppose twenty more rifles were trained on that shadow. But in a moment the shadow said in good American, 'They nicked me a little. Somebody tie up this damn thing for me?'

"We grabbed him. We asked how big a gap the Japs had cut in the line. He laughed. 'What gap? How could the Japs cut through a line of Marines?'

"Well, we woke up to the truth by degrees. Nothing had hit us but a battle rumor. Still, we couldn't relax at once. It took a while before that huddle of black trees at the foot of the hill stopped seeming hostile; it took time to rub the Japs out of the picture and put our men back in, time to realize that all the logical reasoning I'd done about the thin string of Marines and the pressure of Tojo's boys hadn't been worth a damn. Realistically speaking, it was perfectly true. Realistically speaking, we should all have been dead long ago and the Japs sitting around getting drunk on beer and reclaiming all our souvenirs. But it gradually built up in my mind that our fellows down there on the line were maybe a little more than human."

In the morning Guadalcanal remained in American hands, and the pilots and hospital patients who had drawn rifles for the final fight were still alive. More storms were to blow down on the little island, but there was never again a moment so critical. That is the reason the flyers of 212 are glad to point out that while mastery of the air may be important, it is mastery of the ground that decides a war.

# The Coach's Last Flight

*twenty-four*

★The end of the first phase of the war was approaching for members of 212. For some time their commander had been deeply disturbed by their failing health. It's no good sending an airman up to fight against heavy odds when chills may start shaking him at a crucial moment. And now at last the pressure Bauer had been exerting to have his boys relieved took effect. On November 13 the last of his men were on Efate relaxing, getting ready for the trip home, but he had remained behind, as he said, to fix up some odds and ends.

Efate, once a nightmare for Captain Little and his forward echelon, had become a rest camp, a place of happy resort compared with the professional hell on Guadalcanal; but there was nothing on Efate to compare with what waited on the far side of the Pacific for the homeward-bound pilots and ground crew. They had honors coming, but they wouldn't be resting on their laurels. They knew that after a respite in the States they would be reassigned, probably to the Pacific again, some of them perhaps as leaders of new squadrons of Marine flyers. Their unequaled record of ninety-four enemy planes shot down, with a loss of only four of their own, would stand, they hoped, as an inspiration to others, as would the strategies and tactics developed by Bauer for aerial combat and for training and leading pilots. And the knowledge that they had played an honorable part in what might prove a turning point in a global struggle heightened their pride as Marines and as Americans.

November 14 went by comfortably. Next day came news that shrank all their victories and all their thoughts of the future to nothing.

There was one compelling reason why the Coach should have entered on that final danger over Guadalcanal. He had been too long confined to the ground by his duties as commander of the fighter strip. Now that his boys were gone and he was about to have a respite himself, he felt compelled to get into the air one last time. In three contacts with the enemy he had shot down ten planes. Perhaps he hoped to enhance that astonishing record. Anyway, he had at hand an old chum who had risen to the top among American flyers, a perfect companion for the kind of flight he contemplated. That was Captain Joseph J. Foss of Marine Fighter Squadron 121, who was to become one of our leading aces of all time. They were not only friends. Their ideas about air combat meshed fully.

Like most of the younger generation of Marine and Navy fighters, Foss had learned a great deal from Bauer, and with his usual modesty he is the first to admit how much he gained from this teacher. Nothing could be more fitting than that our last notice of Bauer should come through the words of Foss. He wrote to the family of the missing man:

On November 14, 1942, we had heavy enemy action up the line from Guadalcanal. All day we bombed, torpedoed, and strafed their ships by air. Late in the afternoon we had several of their troop transports dead in the water. About four o'clock I received orders to take my flight and escort the dive bombers to that area, and if enemy air activity permitted I was to strafe the transports. Just before I took off, Colonel Joe [Bauer] told me that he was going along and see just how my boys worked. He said I wasn't going to get all the fun alone, so we all took off. Upon arriving there, we found several troop transports dead in the water and smoking. Some warships were cruising among them to pick up survivors and ward off our air attacks. Tom Furlow and I followed the colonel and circled high above. The three of us circled for some time and watched our planes attack and start to leave. All the surrounding air seemed clear from enemy air activity, so down we came and strafed the ships below. We came right out on the water and headed for home. All of a sudden, tracers shot over my head. Upon looking back I saw two Jap Zeros diving on us, shooting. At once, Joe turned and headed straight for one. Both he and the Jap were shooting everything. Then — bang! And the Zero blew up, and Joe zoomed and made a turn for home. Tom and I chased the other Zero toward Tokyo but couldn't catch him. Upon returning to the scene of Joe's action (twelve or fifteen miles due north of the Russell Islands), I was unable to spot him. I saw an oil slick about a mile south of the spot where the Zero had gone in, and upon circling it saw Joe swimming with his life jacket on. I went right down to within a few feet of him, and he waved both arms and jumped up out of the water. Then he waved me toward home. He was in good shape — no visible cuts. I tried to give him my life raft, but it wouldn't come out, so I gave full throttle toward home. I landed and took off at once in a Duck with Major Joe Renner. We were within about ten miles of Joe and it got pitch black, so we had to return home. At daybreak the next morning (Nov. 15) we were on the scene of the colonel's landing with my flight of eight and the Duck. The only thing in sight were two Jap planes, which we shot down at once. We searched and searched the area, but no sign of a soul. We sent up a plane that landed and talked to the natives on the Russell Islands and told them to be on a sharp lookout for

Joe. They found a sergeant pilot that had gone down about five miles farther out than Joe at the same time. It took him about forty-nine hours to make the trip [to the islands], so there is no doubt but what the colonel had the stamina and the heart to make such a swim. So in my way of thinking, one of the following two things happened — either the Japs happened upon him and took him prisoner, or the sharks got him. If the Japs have him, he is safe, in my mind, as he wore his lieutenant colonel's silver oak leaves.

The above is as complete as the action really was.

To me, Marine Corps Aviation's greatest loss in this war is that of Joe. He really had a way all his own of getting a tough job done efficiently and speedily, and was admired by all, from the lowest private to the highest general. I am certain that wherever Joe is today, he is doing things the best way — the Bauer way.

I am hoping that some day Joe will come back — I'll never lose hope, knowing Joe as I did.

VMF-212's embarkation for the States turned from a homeward-bound celebration to an occasion of gloom and sorrow over the disappearance of their leader. It was their philosophy that when a comrade is lost, his name must be X-ed out of the mind during the stress of combat. However, the squadron members had not succeeded in crossing out of their minds the names of Finucane, Hamilton, Haring, and Taylor, while Bauer remained to them a strange mixture of a sense of loss plus something glorious that can never be changed by time or circumstance.

And so he remains to me and, I think, may also remain to all who know the true story of the Coach and his boys. They and their squadron represent values of which we can all be proud, in war as in peace.

# Epilogue and Acknowledgments

Harold William ("Joe") Bauer was posthumously awarded the nation's highest military award, the Medal of Honor, often called the Congressional Medal of Honor. His citation, signed by President Franklin D. Roosevelt, reads:

For conspicuous extraordinary heroism and conspicuous courage as Squadron Commander of Marine Fighting Squadron TWO TWELVE in the South Pacific during the period May 10 to November 14, 1942. Volunteering to pilot a fighter plane in defense of our positions on Guadalcanal, Solomon Islands, Lieutenant Colonel Bauer participated in two air battles against enemy bombers and fighters outnumbering our force more than two-to-one, boldly engaged the enemy and destroyed one Japanese bomber in the engagement of September 28 and shot down four enemy fighter planes in flames on October 3 leaving a fifth smoking badly. After successfully leading twenty-six planes on the over-water ferry flight of more than six hundred miles on October 16, Lieutenant Colonel Bauer, while circling to land, sighted a squadron of enemy planes attacking the *U.S.S. McFarland*. Undaunted by the formidable opposition and with valor above and beyond the call of duty, he engaged the entire squadron and, although alone and his fuel supply nearly exhausted, fought his plane so brilliantly that four of the Japanese planes were destroyed before he was forced down by lack of fuel. His intrepid fighting spirit and distinctive ability as a leader and an airman, exemplified in his splendid record of combat achievement, were vital in the successful operations in the South Pacific Area.

Colonel Bauer's ten-year-old son, William, accepted the medal on behalf of his father in a ceremony at Miramar Naval Air Station, San Diego, California, on May 11, 1946, in the presence of his mother, Harriette H. Bauer, and of Major General Field Harris acting on behalf of General Alexander A. Vandegrift, commander of Marine ground forces on Guadalcanal and later Marine Corps Commandant.

Many members of Marine Fighter Squadron 212 were reassigned to other units after their return to the States in 1942, and some such as Cowboy Stout, John Rogers, and Cloudy Faulkner gave their lives for their country when they returned to the Pacific. Others such as Payne, Drury, Conger, and King survived to achieve distinguished careers in Marine and Navy service, as did Bauer's son, Colonel William D. Bauer, who eventually commanded Squadron 212 among other units during the course of a distinguished, much-decorated career that included duty in Vietnam.

As for 212's Guadalcanal record of ninety-four and a half victories against four losses in two and a half months of intermittent action, it seems to have been unequaled at Guadalcanal or in other theaters of the war, although twenty-five of its victories are sometimes credited to Marine Squadron 223, with whom its members flew at various times. Its helping to sink two Japanese destroyers is borne out by documentation at the Marine Corps Historical Center, Washington, D.C. Such feats form part of the conversation when survivors and friends of the squadron meet today for reunions, and there is a silent moment when they remember "the Coach" and others who are no longer with them. They also think, but do not often speak, of the freedom we enjoy today, thanks greatly to all those like the men of 212 who laid their lives on the line when the crisis came, as it did at Guadalcanal, the turning point of the Pacific war.

My father, Frederick Faust, was proud to know and to work with such men, and he hoped this book would tell others about them. He wanted it — like many others he wrote that reached service men and women and other readers during those wartime years — to be signed with his popular

257

pen name, Max Brand.

When, a year after writing this book, he laid his own life on the line and lost it on a battlefield in Italy, during what he called "the final struggle against Hitlerism," it was among brave men such as these — men whose experiences in whatever part of the world, in whatever period of our history, we need to remember and to understand today, while hoping their sacrifices will never have to be repeated.

On behalf of my father I wish especially to thank Colonel Frank C. Drury, USMC (Ret.), Brigadier General Frederick R. Payne, USMC (Ret.), and Naval Air Reserve Flight Engineer (Ret.) Robert Andrade for their great help in rescuing the manuscript of this book from oblivion and in preparing it for publication. Without them the book would not exist.

I wish also to thank Jon Tuska and Vicki Piekarski, the Marine Corps Historical Center, Anne Collier, Lisle A. Rose, Susan Todd Brook, Mary Lou Kenney, Colonel William D. Bower, USMC (Ret.), John B. Lundstrom, Commander Peter B. Mersky, U.S. Naval Reserve, Major John M. Elliott, USMC (Ret.), The Military Gallery, Sandra K. McDonald, Dorothy R. Goodhart, Chief Warrant Officer Frederick D. Scroggins, USMC (Ret.), Captain George M. Garner, USMC (Ret.), former Marine Technical Sergeant Albert F. Ackerman, Mariette Risley, Mary V. Yates, and my husband, Robert Easton, for their help in making this book possible; and I am grateful to Joe Foss for his helpful endorsement of it.

I also wish especially to thank Henry Cohn who, like my father, was with the 88th Division in Italy in 1944. He knew my father there and, because of that acquaintance, in 1994 set in motion the remarkable series of coincidences that led to publication of *Fighter Squadron at Guadalcanal.*

Spelling and punctuation have been somewhat modified to conform to modern usage while retaining the meaning of the original manuscript.

*Jane Faust Easton*

# Historical Annotations

*Chapter 1.*
**The Forward Echelon**

1. After the Pearl Harbor attack, Japan's major objective in the Pacific was to establish a mid-ocean "ribbon defense line" behind which it could exploit the rich natural resources of South and Southeast Asia. The southern end of this line would be anchored in the eastern Solomon Islands in the Coral Sea directly north of Australia. From bases in the Solomons Japanese air and naval forces could cut the vital supply line from the American West Coast to Australia, thus sealing off the island continent and preparing for its eventual capture. In May 1942 Japanese forces seized the immediately adjacent islands of Guadalcanal and Tulagi and began constructing an airstrip on the former.

   Washington strategists quickly perceived the peril and moved, as swiftly as limited supply and transportation capabilities would allow, to build advance bases on the islands of New Caledonia and the New Hebrides (now part of the Vanuatu Islands group) to check Japanese expansion. The New Hebrides were 500 miles east and south of Guadalcanal; New Caledonia lay 750 miles to the south-southeast.

The spring and early summer of 1942 were thus crucial to both Japan and the United States as the two countries, anticipating impending battle, rushed to complete advance bases at the tip of long, tightly stretched communication and supply lines.

2. During the 1930s the U.S. Marines maintained long-established garrisons at Shanghai and on the Pacific islands of Guam, Wake, and Midway. The islands took on commercial as well as strategic importance after 1935, when Pan American World Airways used them as way stations for its "Clipper" flying boats, which established scheduled runs between San Francisco, Hawaii, Manila, and Macao. Wake and Guam fell to the Japanese during the first days of the war. The author is here referring to men who had returned from island garrison duties in the months and weeks immediately preceding the Pearl Harbor attack.

3. This was apparently a rumor, because the Japanese carrier fleet was hundreds of miles to the west, operating in the New Guinea–Java (Indonesia) area. But it does reflect the apprehensive "Japanese are everywhere" mentality that gripped the U.S. military and civilian populations in the months immediately after Pearl Harbor.

4. The author is referring to one of the most dramatic naval actions of World War II. On

17 December 1939 three British cruisers cornered the German raider *Admiral Graf Spee* off the River Plate and drove her into Montevideo harbor. Seventy-two hours later, by order of Adolf Hitler, the *Admiral Graf Spee* was scuttled outside the harbor by her crew, who were then interned in nearby Argentina. Although the Germans modestly defined the *Admiral Graf Spee* and her two sisters, the *Deutschland* and *Admiral Scheer*, as *Panzerschiffes*, or "armored ships," they were more popularly known in international naval circles as "pocket battleships." With six 11-inch guns and rated at twenty-six knots, the vessels were designed to outshoot any enemy they could not outrun, and cruisers were given little chance against them. Although the *Leander* compiled an enviable war record, she never participated in the Battle of the River Plate. Her sister ship *Achilles* did but was only lightly damaged in her upper works by the guns of the *Admiral Graf Spee*. Throughout the war the *Leander* and *Achilles* were on loan to the Royal New Zealand Navy and were manned by a mixed crew of British officers and petty officers and approximately 375 New Zealand nonrated men.

*Chapter 4.*
## Captain Little's Crisis

1. Will Rogers was a beloved humorist, writer, and actor during the first decades of the cen-

tury. He and Wiley Post, the famous pioneer aviator, were killed in a plane crash at Point Barrow, Alaska, in 1935.

*Chapter 5.*
**First Planes Land on the Strip**

1. The port of Rabaul is on the northwestern tip of the island of New Britain in the western Solomons just north of New Guinea. Rabaul was the main Japanese air and naval base in the Solomons throughout the Guadalcanal campaign and beyond. Rightly considered a very tough "nut" to "crack," it was never captured by the Southwest Pacific Theater forces under Gen. Douglas MacArthur but was instead bypassed and allowed to "rot on the vine." Lae and Salamaua on New Guinea's northwestern coast were less important Japanese staging and supply bases. MacArthur's forces eventually captured them in September 1943.

2. Truk was the main Japanese midocean air and naval base in the Caroline Islands, roughly one thousand miles north and west of Guadalcanal. Like Rabaul, "Japan's Pearl Harbor" was never captured but was neutralized and bypassed.

3. The Japanese lost only one light carrier, the *Shōhō*, in the Battle of the Coral Sea. But the fleet carrier *Shōkaku* was badly damaged, and her sister ship, the *Zuikaku*, lost about half her air group. The Battle of the Coral Sea forced

the Japanese to abandon plans to seize Port Moresby, thus saving Australia from direct and repeated enemy air attacks. Despite loss of the fleet carrier *Lexington*, U.S. officials generally considered the Battle of the Coral Sea a victory, and most historians agree.

*Chapter 7.*
## The Men That Make a Fighter Squadron
1. The famous IFF (identification friend or foe) transmitter was not yet available to front-line pilots in the Pacific.

*Chapter 8.*
## Baptism of Fire
1. The reference is presumably to the Marines' First Raider and First Parachute Battalions amalgamated under Col. Merritt A. Edson.
2. The Tenaru River lay four miles directly east of Henderson Field. The Japanese actually mounted their attack against Marine perimeter defenses on Alligator Creek, several hundred yards east of the airstrip. Under the command of Col. Kiyoano Ichiki, 916 Japanese soldiers attacked Marine lines at 0130 on the morning of 21 August.
3. By 24 August Maj. Gen. Alexander A. Vandegrift commanded about fourteen thousand Marines on Guadalcanal, of whom fewer than one thousand were "raiders" under Edson's command. Throughout the campaign U.S. forces generally outnumbered the Japanese.

But the Marines — and, after 7 October, the Army's Americal Division — remained on the island week after week, while Japanese ground forces were constantly reinforced by the "Tokyo Express": a force of troop transports and supply ships, usually escorted by destroyers and cruisers, that steamed down from Rabaul night after night. The "Cactus Air Force" at Henderson Field was constantly outnumbered by Japanese air units flying down from Rabaul, Buka, and Bunin, and until mid-November the U.S. Navy's forces in the waters surrounding Guadalcanal were inferior to the enemy in both strength and capability.

4. Postwar Japanese accounts confirmed this impression. See, for example, Masatake Okumiya, Jiro Horikoshi, and Martin Caidin, *Zero* (New York: Ballantine Books, 1956), 149.

*Chapter 9.*
**More of 212 Joins the Battle**

1. Conger understandably romanticized Navy life in general and carrier life in particular. During the first year of the war, as the United States rapidly geared up to fight a two-front global conflict, the supply situation in the South Pacific, as elsewhere, was abominable. When the men of VMF-212 joined her, the *Wasp* had just completed a week's reprovisioning at Noumea. But before that time, while sailing for five weeks on patrol south of Guadalcanal, the ship's company had been subsisting on

"block beef" (i.e., Spam) and dumplings.

2. At 1500 on 15 September, three torpedoes from the Japanese submarine *I-19* instantly transformed the *Wasp* into a blazing wreck. As "duty carrier," the *Wasp* had just launched a combat air patrol when the torpedoes exploded. All fuel lines and ammunition boxes were open throughout the hangar and flight decks.

3. Maj. Loftus Henderson.

## Chapter 12.
## An Encounter with the Japanese Navy

1. The action actually took place on 11 October.
2. Actually Alligator Creek
   (see note 2 to chap. 8).

## Chapter 13.
## VMF-212's Mechanics Build a New Air Force

1. The Battle of Cape Esperance was fought on the night of 11–12 October between a Japanese bombardment group consisting of three cruisers and eight destroyers and the U.S. Navy's Task Force 64, commanded by Rear Adm. Norman Scott and comprising four cruisers and five destroyers. The Americans claimed their first naval victory of the Guadalcanal campaign, sending one Japanese heavy cruiser and three destroyers to the bottom in exchange for the loss of one destroyer and damage to two cruisers.

*Chapter 14.*
**Darkest Hours**

1. MacArthur was not responsible for Guadalcanal, which was in the domain of Adm. Robert L. Ghormley, commander of the U.S. Forces South Pacific. Ghormley was broken by the early October crises on and around the island and was relieved on 18 October by Adm. William F. "Bull" Halsey, much to the relief and joy of all hands. Halsey promptly issued an order, "KILL JAPS, KILL JAPS, KILL MORE JAPS," which was soon displayed prominently at the small fleet landing on Tulagi across the sound from Guadalcanal.

2. These missions were actually flown from the carrier *Hornet* because incessant enemy bombing and shelling had temporarily knocked out Henderson Field. The brief respite provided by the *Hornet*'s fliers, and Bauer's reinforcement that evening with the remainder of VMF-212, allowed the Cactus Air Force to recover quickly and regain the initiative in the skies over Guadalcanal.

*Chapter 19.*
**Fireworks over Guadalcanal**

1. This and the following chapter describe aerial operations conducted in conjunction with the celebrated — and doomed — effort by the Sendai Division, under the command of Lt. Gen. Harukichi Hyakutake, to finally end the

Guadalcanal campaign by capturing Henderson Field and driving the Marines into the sea. The Japanese Navy's ill-coordinated, bumbling efforts to support the Sendai offensive with a decisive thrust against the small U.S. carrier fleet near Guadalcanal resulted in the Battle of Santa Cruz, in which the Americans lost the *Hornet* and the Japanese suffered severe damage to two of their four carriers. Although not mentioned here, Hyakutake's offensive reached the edge of Henderson Field during the night of 25–26 October before the Americans forced the Japanese back and nearly wiped out the Sendai Division. See also note 1 to chap. 23.

*Chapter 20.*
**One Day in the Life of Jack Conger**

1. Although several Japanese warships were sunk or damaged by Cactus Air Force bombs that day, none was sunk by machine-gun fire alone.

2. The Japanese pilot was Shiroamao Ishikawa, who spent the remainder of the war in a New Zealand prisoner-of-war compound. After returning to Japan, Ishikawa completed his education and worked for thirty years in the Tokyo office of the Chase Manhattan Bank. According to historian Richard B. Frank's *Guadalcanal*, Ishikawa and Conger met again in Texas in 1990, forty-eight years after their first encounter in the waters off Guadalcanal.

*Chapter 23.*

## A Memorable Night on "the Canal"

1. It seems likely that Sgt. DeBenedictis was actually describing the assault of the Sendai Division on Henderson Field during the night of 25–26 October (see note 1 to chap. 19). The last major Japanese effort to reinforce Guadalcanal and destroy Vandegrift's forces was foiled by the great naval battles in adjacent "Ironbottom Sound" on the nights of 13 November and 14–15 November. The Japanese lost two battleships, one heavy cruiser, and three destroyers and were so disheartened that they turned most of their attention and resources to strengthening their forces on New Guinea. By mid-December the Japanese were preparing to abandon Guadalcanal.

*Lisle A. Rose*

The employees of G.K. Hall hope you have enjoyed this Large Print book. All our Large Print titles are designed for easy reading, and all our books are made to last. Other G.K. Hall books are available at your library, through selected bookstores, or directly from us.

For information about titles, please call:

(800) 223-2336

To share your comments, please write:

Publisher
G.K. Hall & Co.
P.O. Box 159
Thorndike, ME  04986